Sri Prem Baba

PURPOSE

The courage to be who we are

Table of Contents

Introduction

Perhaps the greatest misfortune that has ever affected human beings was to have believed at some point on their journey that they were the center of creation. Our intelligence has brought us many conquests. We have gained a certain control of matter, and as a result, began to act as if nature existed only to serve us. The ego, as a symbol of individuality, took over our experience on Earth. This limited view led us to forget who we are and what we came here to do. We are now suffering from a serious illness called egoism that leads us to display an unbearable level of disrespect for nature and other human beings as well as a profound ignorance about the meaning of life.

We have used our intelligence over the centuries to reaffirm this self-centered view and prove we are superior to everything and everybody. The ego, which is only a vehicle for the experience of the soul on this terrestrial plane, became the one who rules everything, and individualism took on brutal proportions. We have lost the connection with our spiritual identity and the very reason why we are here. We have stopped wondering about the meaning of life and this has made us forget our essence and its intrinsic values.

The theory that the universe is the product of a cosmic accident (the Big Bang) upholds the materialistic view that life has no purpose. If we are the product of an accident, we are here by chance. And if we are here by chance, there is no point in our existence. However, this idea stems from our inability to explain what is behind the mystery of creation through scientific methods. This is what leads us to deny the spirit and believe that there is nothing beyond the body and matter. However, this materialism is what has prevented our growth, not only spiritually but also materially! This is because, by taking this approach, we are becoming blinder and more ignorant in relation to our own power.

The idea that we are only a body, combined with the belief that we are superior to everything, is what makes us indifferent in the face of the destruction of our planet and skeptical in relation to spirituality. Setting aside discoveries made by physics that are not even that recent, we continue to foster a solely materialistic view of life. As individuals and society, we continue to deny the existence of a single spirit that gives life and interconnects all living beings and nature.

However, all this is part of the challenges of human experience on Earth, as we are here precisely to grasp the memory of who we are and what we came to do. Although forgetfulness is a learning tool in this game of life, it becomes a great obstacle to the expansion of consciousness when taken to an extreme, and humanity is currently in its grip. Most people do not have the slightest idea of what they have come here to do and do not even get around to ask themselves this question.

We are now approaching a critical point in which a turnaround is needed. It is as if we were approaching the end of a large project and were being pressurized to comply with our mission. Some say that the final deadline has already passed and there is nothing more we can do. Others believe that we still have the chance of achieving our goal. I believe we need to undergo great transformations if we are to be successful. Firstly, we need to open ourselves up to the truth that we are spiritual beings living a material experience on Earth and that we all have a common mission—because without this awareness we are doomed to extinction.

Who am I?
What have I come here for?

It is part of our mission to reach the answer to these questions. We are constantly being encouraged to ask and find answers to questions like these and invited to perceive and understand the Mystery. Nature has sent very clear messages that the time has arrived for us to awaken from the dream of forgetfulness and wake up to reality. With so much information available on the unsustainable nature of our lifestyle, it is no longer acceptable for us to continue to act without a minimum of environmental awareness. It is now inconceivable that we are still so skeptical and closed that we cannot perceive the greater reality that transcends matter, since it is this shut-down state that prevents us from having access to the purpose of life.

I, as a spiritual master, but above all, as a conscientious human being, have the obligation to tell the truth, no matter how painful it might be: we human beings are heading for a great failure. We have been unable to find this so desired happiness until this point in our passage here on Earth. This is because we are looking in the wrong place—outside ourselves. Happiness does not lie in the future, in material goods, or in the opinion other people have of us. It is here and now, inside us.

We need to have the courage and humility to give up our pride and take responsibility for our mistakes. We need to cure ourselves of egoism and only self-knowledge can bring about this cure. It was precisely with the intention of offering instruments that allow and facilitate the process of self-knowledge but, above all, with the aim of giving movement to an energy that can drive a real transformation that I decided to write this book.

Each and every one of us has come to this earthly plane with a mission, a purpose to be fulfilled. Despite the fact that on the surface we are not equal and have different qualities, we are united in one unique purpose that, at the end of the day, is the expansion of consciousness. Consciousness expands through love. That is why I often say that our work as human beings is to awaken love in everyone, everywhere.

We can compare the process of the expansion of consciousness to the growth of a tree. The root represents our memories, our inheritance, our ancestors, i.e. our story on Earth. It keeps us grounded and doesn't allow us to fall. It is the root that supports the tree trunk, which in turn represents our consolidated values and virtues. The stronger the trunk the higher we can reach. The branches represent the development of our virtues in gifts and talents; the leaves represent life's driving force and our eternal capacity for renewal. And when we manage to turn ourselves into channels of love through our gifts and talents, flowers and fruits bloom representing exactly what we came to undertake, offer, or deliver to the world. The flowers and fruits represent the manifestation or the realization of our life's purpose.

I now want to invite you to embark with me on a journey towards the expansion of consciousness. It is an adventure full of uncertainty and challenges that will take us from the seed to the fruit, from Earth to heaven, from forgetfulness to remembrance, from being asleep to the state of an awake consciousness. It is a journey that reveals the infinite unfoldings of love—this power that inhabits us, moves us and liberates us.

Love is the seed, the sap and the flavor of the fruit. It is the beauty and the fragrance of the flower. The beginning, the middle and the end. Awakening love is the reason why we are here.

May the message contained in this book serve as an inspiration and guide for your journey.

1. Birth

A POTENTIAL IS BORN

To make a journey on this physical plane we need a means of transport. For the soul to move towards divine consciousness, we need to pass through human consciousness. In order to go through this experience here on Earth, benefiting from a human personality, the spirit needs a vehicle, because it would be unable to cope with this experience without an ego and a body. Therefore, we are born with a body and a psychological structure created to develop an ego. Ego and body form a vehicle, an instrument created in such a way that the spirit can undergo this material experience.

Principle of the idea of "I"

The soul is the individual portion of the spirit that manifests itself through this vehicle. It is the bridge between the material and spiritual planes. The soul follows the Being throughout its evolutionary journey, through cycles of death and rebirth, and ceases to exist when the individual consciousness expands and merges into the cosmic consciousness.

This is the way that consciousness finds to expand itself through the human being on the material plane. Just as a plant is born and grows from a seed, the cosmic consciousness shows itself and expands through an individual consciousness

In this sense, the ego is like a seed that is planted in the ground with the aim of growing, maturing and producing fruit. This seed brings with it a divine potential that will express itself in a particular way through each one of us.

There are many definitions of the word ego. When I use it here I am referring to it as the principle of individuation or also the principle of the idea of "I." Although the ego has a very important function in the divine project of expanding consciousness (the goal of which, at the end of the day, is to re-establish a state of Unity), it also represents the birth of a sense of separation, i.e. it is the principle of the idea that we are separate, one from the other. As we have a body, a form, the mind creates this illusion of separation. At the physical level, which is the level of appearances, we are actually separated, but we are one at the level of the spirit.

However, this illusion is part of the divine game here on Earth and is at the service of the expansion of consciousness. It is what in the Hindu cosmic view is called *mahamaya*, the great illusion. At the same time as it covers our view with the veil of duality, *mahamaya* is also our great teacher. Through it we learn what we need to learn and gradually we begin to see beyond it. *Mahamaya* is a distortion of reality that can take many forms, including egoism—the illness of the ego.

Seeds of love

When we allow ourselves to contemplate and become involved in the beauty of life, observing the phenomena of nature, we notice everything is fantastic and that life certainly goes well beyond this daily reality we capture through our physical eyes. Have you ever wondered how it is possible that fruits and flowers of the most varied sizes, colors, fragrances and flavors simply grow from trees? This is fantastic. Even if you know how nature operates, if you can observe these phenomena in greater depth, you will immediately see how extraordinary it is. A seed is an example of this. From a small grain, a majestic tree grows. The seed contains a minimum portion within itself, a quantum of an essence that is printed in a genetic code. This code contains the information on its maximum potential, which is also what it will carry out when it is planted in the earth. Its maximum potential is the fruit it will produce.

Similarly, we human beings bring a portion of divine consciousness that wants to expand and express itself through us. We also bring a code, a program, something to be fulfilled. This program is the purpose of the soul. We came to this world precisely to carry out this purpose, which I also usually call vision—a vision to be shared with the world.

The purpose manifests itself in a very particular way in each one of us. Each individual soul arrives here with a specific program to be carried out and this program or individual purpose is aligned with the greatest purpose of life. I am referring to what in the ancient wisdom of yoga is known as *dharma*—the universal law that governs life and unites all beings around the same purpose. In the last instance, *dharma* or humanity's greatest purpose, is the expansion of consciousness. However, I usually call it the awakening of love, since consciousness expands itself through it.

If we know the purpose, then we know what we came here for. And what we came here to do is intimately related to that which we are in essence, i.e. the individual program of the soul is related to the consciousness of the Being. Just as a orange tree can only produce oranges, the human being can only produce one kind of fruit: love, since love is its essence. However, love is a fruit that can show itself in infinite ways. Every soul brings within gifts and talents that are the unique way in which love expresses itself through us.

Challenges of growth

At the same time as each soul brings gifts and talents with it, which are its virtues and potentials to be developed, it also brings challenges that will serve for its growth. Certain challenges are part of the very program of the soul and are printed in the DNA, such as genetic diseases and physical limitations. Others will be created from the choices a soul makes during its incarnation. However, the challenges are tools of learning regardless of their nature.

I also compare these challenges or obstacles to stopping places on the developing soul's journey. It is a long one and we often feel tired. Sometimes, we need to stop and regain our energy and eat, at times to fulfill agreements in specific places. But every stop serves in some way to allow us to recover and absorb what we have learned. The stopovers help us review the map of life and find out where we are on the journey. During these moments, we can also review the places where we have been and the holes where we've passed over in order to prevent new falls. However, we stop mainly to rescue parts of ourselves that have become trapped in the past and to absorb certain lessons. By doing so, we gradually gain strength to follow the route to the final destination.

These stopping places where the soul parks temporarily to absorb certain lessons and free itself from the chain of reactions, created by mistaken actions in the past, are what we call *karma*. This Sanskrit word literally means "action" but it refers to a cosmic law—the law of cause and effect (action and reaction). This states that every effect has a cause: everything that shows itself in our lives now is a product of our actions in the past. For every action, there is a reaction. Therefore, *karma* involves not only the action but also the inherent reaction to it.

One kind of yoga, called *Karma Yoga* (the yoga of action), speaks about the practice of "non-action," which is an action that does not create reaction—a cause without effect. However, for an action not to create any reaction, it needs to be deprived of egoistic interests. This is the basic foundation of *Karma Yoga* (yoga of action), the principal instrument of which is detached action or service.

A lot is spoken about yoga nowadays but very little is really known about it. Yoga is not simply a system of physical postures and meditation. Yoga is a great combination of techniques and tools that can act in all levels of our system (physical, mental, psycho-emotional, energetic and spiritual) and has the function of helping us to reconnect with the greater reality, with our essence and also with our true identity. Therefore, yoga is a way of self-realization or liberation. When we recognize our true identity, we become free to be who we are.

Karma Yoga is the road to freedom through action; it is the kind of yoga that leads to self-realization through selfless service. Selfless action frees us, as it allows us to stop producing reactions and, subsequently, to free ourselves from the web of *karma*. But this is only possible when *karma* (action) and *dharma* (purpose) are aligned, which means that our actions correspond to what we really came here for. The more aligned they are with the greater purpose, the fewer effects our actions will cause and they will bring more consciousness to the planet since the purpose of the individual soul is directly linked to the collective *dharma* and *karma*.

EXTERNAL INFLUENCES

We saw that there is an internal purpose (of the soul), a program that is born with the person. However, there is also another purpose, which is external—a program that is formed during life, along with the development of the ego and through contact with society. This program, which is drawn up based on external influences, is what I will call here the "ego program."

The ego program not only depends on external factors but will also depend on *karma* as that is what determines the conditions in which the child arrives on this earthly plane. Depending on the social conditions, level of knowledge and spiritual development of the family, the child may learn some kind of lessons, develop particular skills and consolidate values and virtues of the soul. At the same time, the child might experience traumas and create images (fixed or frozen psychological scenarios) and limiting beliefs that will be part of this programming.

The purpose of the ego, or external purpose, is like the peel of a fruit and is a layer on the surface that covers up the real program of the soul. However, the peel also has a function and serves as a protection to allow the ego to develop and build what is necessary for its experience. But a moment arrives when this outside layer needs to be removed so the true purpose can manifest itself fully. Just as we need to remove the peel of the fruit to enjoy it, so this external program needs to be removed for the internal program to reveal itself.

The human entity arrives on this terrestrial plane free, loving and trusting. When it is born, the child still has a recollection of who it is and what it has come here for. However, with the passing of time, through the contact with the world, the child gives in to the outside influences, acquiring beliefs and repressing its natural expression. As we know, the base of the personality is formed during the first seven years of life. Some characteristics are acquired later, in the following seven years, but the foundation is made in the first seven years and the beliefs installed in this period will permeate the person's whole life.

So the child begins to feel deprived and insecure at a very early stage. It starts to feel jealousy, anger and envy . . . and this does not happen by chance. The child learns this from people around it, particularly the parents but also from teachers and other close relatives. These people take part in the process of developing the personality of that soul. They unwittingly end up transferring their woes and neediness onto the child. This leads to a vicious circle in which ignorance procreates ignorance.

When the child begins to go to school and starts a social life, it receives new inputs (besides those that come via the parents and relatives) about what is supposedly right or wrong, on what it should be and do in life (which is usually not what the child would like to be and do). New limits and rules are imposed and new ideas (prejudices, opinions, beliefs are conveyed. Obviously, limits and rules are needed for the child's own good, but no one teaches that certain rules will need to be abandoned as they should be at the service of the development of consciousness and not the opposite.

Every human being brings a view in favor of the sustainable development of the planet with it. He or she brings a wisdom, a power. However, as a result of these outside influences, this view is gradually forgotten, and its power gets reined in. As this power is reined in, it turns against the human being, and forces that go against his or her purpose are created. The program of the soul impels the person to move in one direction but the mind conditioned by outside factors makes the person follow another. This contradiction creates suffering.

Forgetting the vision

We can say, in a synthetic way, that we are here to carry out a journey from the state of forgetfulness to the state of remembrance—remembering who we are and what we have come here for—since, as we have seen, on arriving on this Earth, we are wrapped in a veil of illusion that operates by amnesia.

People usually have a clear view of what they have come to do until the beginning of adolescence: they carry a strong wish, they bring in them dreams that are expressions of their purpose. However, these are gradually forgotten. Adolescents gradually start believing in external voices, which insist on saying that this is an impossible dream that cannot be realized, that this road is not good and also that the person is not capable of doing such a thing. They gradually give in to these voices until they give up and completely forget their dreams and start to dream other people's dreams.

If you have ever had the opportunity to follow the growth of a child, you know it is born trusting and loving in the purest way. The child, which has still not been corrupted and contaminated by the beliefs and afflictions of the adults around it, simply holds the hand of its father and mother and goes with them without knowing where it is being led. However, the child gradually stops having this trust and starts being struck by fear in the shape of wariness and insecurity and by hate in the form of anger and vengeance.

But why does this happen? Because the child is taught that. The child learns from an early age that it is a victim of outside circumstances and, as a result, it also learns that it needs to defend itself. It gradually acquires the most varied mechanisms of defense and beliefs and restraints. These mechanisms are limiting because although they serve for protection, they also create separation and forgetfulness. The walls you build around yourself for protection are the very ones that keep you isolated from the world.

This combination of protection mechanisms and forgetfulness make up what I usually call "inferior nature", "lower self", and also "evil." What we call evil is nothing more than a grouping of defense mechanisms human beings develop from an early age to protect themselves from the pain of the shocks of humiliation, rejection and exclusion. When speaking of evil, I am not referring only to the behavior of criminals and those who are corrupt, since all of us have gone through shocks of this kind. Therefore, all of us are carrying some evil within us, and the more evil a person shows, the more pain he or she carries within his or her system.

Contamination by education

Obviously, education plays a major role in the formation of the child's personality as well as in the process of expanding human consciousness. This process can be made easier or harder through education. This is why we should give due importance to this issue. I believe it is only through education that we can trigger the transformation that is needed to save our planet from the process of degradation it is currently in. However, for any significant change to occur, we need to carry out a great reform in education and this reform begins with us adults.

The process of educating our children should begin by reeducating our lower self. This is the only way in which we will really have something to give. If not, what we call education will continue to be just a reaction to the past and only a projection of our childhood pains. We are projecting our woes onto the children and we want to shape them into what we consider the best. However, we are not always right about what is the best precisely because we are dealing with a belief, i.e. a fixed image of something. Belief is built on negative situations from the past. This means that something went wrong and something hurt you, then you started to believe that life is always like that. This is a generalization.

Therefore, we face a great challenge ahead. We need to cure our woes so we can educate our children properly because, if we continue to act based on our own traumas, we will continue to undermine our children's development and divert them from their natural path and their purpose in life. This will only be possible if we are ready to assume our responsibility and get to know ourselves because by knowing ourselves, we will free ourselves from the beliefs that restrain us and the idea that we are victims. We will then be able to support the sustainable development of the child's personality, which means not projecting our anxieties onto the children and providing the strength that enables the children's vision and wisdom to be revealed to the world.

We have to give up the need to have our expectations and neediness fulfilled through our children as this is the root of the problem. I know it is no easy task as it is very difficult not to repeat patterns and impose points of view on the child. Not knowing your own self and having no awareness of your own neediness and limitations means that you will inevitably want to shape the child in line with your expectation. If you were badly hurt, deprived and humiliated, it is very likely that, once you are in a position of power and authority over the child, you will become lost and want to abuse this false power. By doing so, you end up re-editing your past in the present time, which means that you are repeating your own life story through the child and transmitting your miseries to it.

The projection of our neediness and conditionings onto our children is one of the bases that maintain human misery. By doing so, we have been channels of a destructive power that encourages us to forget life's greater purpose. The child tries to be happy in the way we teach it to be but it never feels that it fits in; it doesn't feel comfortable. The child is taken over by forgetfulness from an early age and starts to bear an existential void of which it is unaware, until a certain stage.

Lost in forgetfulness, the child believes that this void (from which it is always unconsciously trying to flee) will be filled with something from outside. The child believes its happiness depends on outside circumstances, i.e. from other people or material goods. As a result, it ends up developing the belief that happiness can be bought. The child believes that if it has a lot of money, not only will it be able to buy everything it desires but it will be able to dominate the other person and make that person give the child what it expects.

Our educational system is based on this: teaching the child to gain money and have power precisely because our society is founded on this belief that money is synonymous with happiness. Nothing could be more misleading than this. It is because of this great illusion that depression has become the illness of the century and that we have become dependent on drugs to sleep and alleviate anxiety. We are creating a humanity that is dependent on therapy. There is also no guarantee that we will resolve the problem even with therapy. There are people who do therapy throughout their entire lives and remain the same. Many manage to live better, accept themselves more and take some steps on the path of self-knowledge but it is only through spirituality that we can break with this vicious circle. Therapeutic processes can only bring positive results in terms of healing our roots (where the illness is installed) if they can address and treat the human being as a whole, including his or her spiritual dimension.

This prospect needs to be changed. If not, then we will continue procreating unhappiness. It is up to us adults to free ourselves from these restraining beliefs and begin the search for happiness in the right place: inside ourselves. This is the only place where long-lasting happiness can be found. As long as we continue to look outside, projecting our neediness onto others, demanding that they do what we want them to, while we do not cure our own childhood injuries through self-knowledge, we will continue to procreate ignorance through our children.

You often think you are loving your child, but you are only trying to resolve your own problem. You are actually trying to fulfill yourself through your child. By forcing the children to do things your way, you end up diverting them from their way. And any path that is not that of the soul is a bad path because it will be moving away from *dharma*.

If we could prevent these beliefs being implanted in childhood everything would be different. I believe this would be possible if self-knowledge and spirituality become part of primary education. As conscientious adults, our work is to rescue the lost innocence, the spontaneity and the purity of the child in us since we can then also rescue the joy and lightness of living. But as long as this is not happening, may we strive to ensure our children do not lose their innocence and spontaneity. This is a project that will last for centuries, but we need to start on it now. We need to make an education based on human and spiritual values become public policy. It is also essential that lovers become truly aware of what a family means, what bringing a child into this world really means. This is one of the aspects of our mission on this planet because it is part of the process of the expansion of human consciousness.

If we look more closely at this question, we will even see that we need to reflect on our compulsive need to have children as it also arises from beliefs and conditionings. I notice that this topic is almost taboo in our society, but it is an issue of great importance that has to be tackled head on and faced. This is because, by bringing a child into this world, you have the responsibility for helping in the spiritua development of this soul or at least you have to learn how not to undermine it.

These are very important questions, but we would need another book to deal with them. For the time being, I only want to leave some questions for those who wish to have children. Who in you wants to have a child and what for? Where does this wish come from? Does it come from the need to fulfil a social program, to fill a void or is it a command from the heart?

Poisons for the consciousness

I repeat that this transformation, which is so necessary and challenging, can only occur if we are really committed to self-knowledge. And this includes studying the mechanisms that lead us to forget the real purpose of life. We have to know how we have been contaminated by fear; how our natural trust has been transformed into mistrust; how the beliefs and conditionings have been established within our system, setting off the vicious circles that generate destruction and perpetuate misery, not only in our personal lives but also in the life of the planet as a whole.

Identifying these vicious circles and understanding how they work gives us the chance to interrupt them. When this happens, the energy that has been used to uphold the forgetfulness until that time can be redirected and we can remember who we are.

The main mechanisms which are behind forgetfulness are repression and denial. They act like real poisons attacking consciousness within our system. Let us see how:

Repression

As I mentioned earlier, when a human entity is born, although it still has a memory of its identity, it shows limits that make it dependent. Therefore, it needs to receive many things from its parents, of which three elements are the most vital: food, protection and love. These are basic elements so the child can survive and grow in a healthy way. Furthermore, there is another element that is also essential, but which is usually ignored: freedom. Freedom is as basic a need for the soul as food is for the body. In fact, it is intrinsic to the Being, but when we are incarnated on this plane our freedom is restricted.

When we arrive here, we are pure and have no fear or shame of being who we are. We see no danger or malice in anything, which is why we express ourselves with total freedom, spontaneity and naturalness. However, this natural expression of ours is not always regarded as being socially adequate and often does not correspond to our parents' expectations for us. The fact is that in most cases, the parents are not mature enough to accept and receive the child's spontaneity and allow it to express itself with the freedom it needs.

Therefore, the child starts being repressed from an early age and comes into contact with the feeling of inadequacy this creates. Sometimes the child is repressed in a direct, open way when told "don't do this!" or "this is not allowed!" while at others it occurs in an indirect and subtle way through the removal of love. If the child does something the parents do not like or regard as inadequate, the child is punished by being treated coldly and indifferently. On some occasions, the child is beaten or humiliated.

When sexuality begins to arise, and the child starts to play with its own body, the first thing it usually hears is: "Stop that! It's dirty!" The child is there, pure, without any malice and simply being spontaneous, but it is repressed in this natural movement and its vital energy is suddenly blocked. As a result, the child begins to be afraid of being who they are and starts believing it should be something else to please its parents and receive what it needs. The child ceases to be spontaneous and begins to create masks, i.e. the child starts to pretend they are something they are not because acting as they actually are does not get them what they want, which is being accepted and loved. This leads to a false identity being created.

Spontaneity starts giving way to strategy, which means the child no longer follows its heart but starts to behave in a way that pleases others. The child stops listening to the heart and replaces it with the mind. Reason takes over from intuition, but reason without intuition is the same as a bird without wings. By acting purely based on reason and rationality, you become a machine, and by acting based only on feeling and instinct, you become an animal. Intuition brings together thinking and feeling, reasoning and instinct. It brings us closer to what defines us as human beings.

Understand that I am not saying that the mind and reason are to be ignored. In fact, the mind is a power of the Being, but this power has been used very badly. In the current stage of our evolutionary journey, the mind finds itself completely out of control, creating difficulties and obstacles for human consciousness to develop. There must be a balance between the mind and the heart, between reason and intuition, as this is what allows us to transcend our limitations and achieve our potential.

It is also important to make clear the difference between that which I call repression and the limits needed for education and the child's protection. Obviously, the child needs limits, even for its own protection. The child often even asks for limits since this is a way in which the parents will give it attention. The limit, if set with love and awareness, is a means of helping the child's development. Repression is the opposite. It is like a poison that acts by contaminating a virtue that constitutes the base, the foundation of the tree of consciousness—self-confidence. Spontaneity, which is an expression of self-confidence, is blocked and contaminated by fear, the fear of not receiving love. This is the basic illusion that upholds unhappiness in the world: the idea that we are needy and we need to receive something from outside.

Denial

The distancing from our true identity becomes greater and greater until it reaches a point when a split occurs: we lose the connection with what we are and start believing we are the mask. This split is extremely painful and feels as if we have been cut in two or a hole has opened up inside us. This is what originates the great inner void that accompanies the human being throughout its existence, and we trigger the mechanism of denial to cope with this brutal pain.

Just as we relieve the pain of physical wounds with analgesics, so we ease the emotional injuries by denial. Denial is like a psycho-emotional painkiller that can act for an undetermined time. It is a mechanism that can send all the negative feelings and all the internal content we do not want to see and feel to the deepest parts of the unconsciousness

This is how we hide what we do not accept and do not wish to come into contact with from others and ourselves.

This is the way we find to protect ourselves and no longer come into contact with the reality that we have been repressed and hurt. This mechanism sustains the false identity because it strengthens the unconscious belief that we are needy victims who are not accepted for what we really are.

The unconscious, also known in psychology as the subconscious, is a part of the consciousness that we do not want to see for some reason. It is not something we really do not know but something that, at some point, we decided not to know. Just as we were born naturally loving and we gradually learnt to hate (or unlearnt to love), everything that became unconscious was, at some time, within the light of consciousness. Therefore, what I usually call the "lower self" or "shadow" is precisely this portion of the consciousness we choose not to see and, for this reason, we have switched off the light. Switching off the light means closing the heart and closing the heart means disconnecting from oneself.

This disconnection created by the split with the true identity creates the illusion that we are separated from the source of life. In other words, we lose awareness of the source of life residing in us and that we are part of a current of universal energy from which we receive everything we need. As we believe we are separated from this source that nurtures us, we start believing we are needy and, as a result, become slaves of the other. The source of love is within us, but we believe that we need to receive this love from someone else.

The denial of the dark aspects of the personality is perhaps the main cause of human misery. The feelings that have been denied operate as anchors that prevent rising. The hurt and resentment we are burdened with, even unconsciously, keep us prisoners of the illusion of separation, distorting the perception of reality and preventing us from showing our power in the form of our gifts and talents. As a result, we are prevented from achieving the greater purpose, which is the memory of who we are and of what we have come here for.

2. Growth

FALSE IDENTITY

Every being who is incarnated on this earthly plane undergoes this rupturing process I have just described. It is part of the challenges we need to face up to during the incarnation. A false identity is created as a result of this split with our true identity. To maintain this false identity, we develop a real aggressive arsenal made up of various defense mechanisms and their extensive unfoldings.

Guardians of the false Self

The main mechanisms the ego uses to maintain the false identity are the matrices of the lower Self. I have spoken a lot about this aspect, including in my previous books, but it is worth repeating:

Gluttony – This represents every kind of voraciousness or compulsion; these are the most gross or dense, the most concrete addictions, the easiest to identify and study. They can include a compulsion to eat, buy things, speak, and have sex, among other things. At the foundation of this matrix lies the belief that, by consuming or swallowing a certain element, you will fill the neediness and the existential void. Compulsion stems from neediness and arises from the cut of the connection with the essence through repression. The glutton tries to fill in the hole created by the split with food or any other element that can replace the lack of love. This need creates a voraciousness that is transformed into anxiety when it is not met.

Sloth – This is paralysis in the face of what needs to be done as a result of the feelings that are suppressed and frozen in the system. Sloth can appear in a passive or active way. When it appears in passive form, people fail to do what they should (at times they cannot even get out of bed). This creates an imbalance in the chemistry of the brain and leads to depression. When it appears in an active form, the person does a lot (sometimes becoming a workaholic) except what really needs to be done.

Greed – This is the need to accumulate things, and people protect themselves through the things they accumulate. They believe they will be safeguarded by accumulating things. Some hide themselves behind money, but there are people who conceal themselves behind discarded old things they find in the street or even collect garbage. They accumulate and are unable to throw anything away, not even an old nail.

Envy – This represents the desire to destroy the other person in the belief that this person is superior. The envious person does not believe he or she is capable of arriving where the other person has and, therefore, needs to diminish this person. To do this, he or she disparages and speaks badly about the other. This disparagement can be very strong or carried out in subtler ways that are difficult to identify. For example, if you are in an area in which the person you envy is highly regarded and admired, you decide to inject a dash of poison and speak badly of this person as though praising him or her: "She is a very nice person. Pity about that fault."

There is also another aspect of envy that is difficult to understand: self-envy. This is an aspect that is connected to pride and lust. When self-envy is at work, the person begins to sabotage his or her own self. In this case, the situation is more complicated because it is an aspect that is extremely difficult to identify.

Rage – This is an extreme reaction to situations. The person who displays this matrix believes he or she will be protected by speaking louder than the other. He shouts and intimidates the other person in order to feel stronger, conveying the idea that he is very brave whereas in fact he is scared to death.

Pride – It uses superiority to feel protected. From pride onwards, matrices start becoming more sophisticated as they act in subtler and subtler ways. Although all matrices have their complexities, the previous ones are relatively easier to deal with (except self-envy). Pride is complex because it can appear in many different forms. Some examples are vanity, arrogance, shyness, inferiority or superiority complex, acting like a victim and false humility.

Lust – This is the need to obtain power through sexual energy. Lust is not always linked to sex in itself but the use of seduction, which can occur in various ways. The need to please the other person is often a way of dominating them. Lust is intimately connected to rage as it transforms itself into rage when it does not get what it wants.

Fear – There are many beliefs linked to fear. Fear is at the foundation of the structure of the lower self and upholds the illusion that we are needy and are only a body. Fear is the antithesis of love.

Lie – This is the subtlest of the matrices because lying is not just what you say on a daily basis to "look good", but it is also what supports all other matrices. The biggest lie at the end of the day is the one you tell yourself: the lie about your real identity.

Masks

If you believe you are needy, you will unavoidably expect to receive something from the other. You will end up having expectations. This is a big problem because you have no guarantees that you will receive what you want, no matter how wonderful you are. No matter how skilled you are in convincing the other person to give what you think you need to receive, you have no guarantee that the person will match your expectation.

Although everything you are pursuing outside yourself is actually inside you, you cannot see this reality. The Being that lives within you is complete and needs nothing, but your perception is limited by conditionings and beliefs, so you are unable to see that reality. That is why you become a beggar and sell your soul for a crumb of attention. You pretend to be what you are not and use masks to please people and receive a little gaze or look, a bit of affection. By doing so, you waste your life trying to force the other person to love you. This is a state of imprisonment, of great dependence, which creates anger and this anger turns against you.

You feel angry because you somehow know that you are selling yourself out. You are prostituting yourself. Once when someone was making a judgment on prostitution thought "who in this world does not pay for sex?" Prostitute at least make the price very clear. Forgive my frankness but I need to be honest. My job is to eliminate the lie and feed the truth. Just think: who does not pay to receive attention? Who does not pay to receive affection?

As you are involved in the idea of neediness, you pay with your spontaneity and freedom. You stop being who you really are and specialize in being anything that steals the attention of the other. You specialize in taking energy from the other person and creating strategies to keep hold of it. This is slavery!

Sometimes, you put on the mask of a victim to attract attention: "I will kill myself if you don't look at me." Sometimes the disguise is one of self-sufficiency: "I don't need you. I am strong and can look after my own life." Other times, you simply use indifference: "I couldn't care less. I am above all this." These examples are the classic patterns, but each one has endless unfoldings. They are only a sample of what you do to conquer, dominate and manipulate the other person in line with your need to be loved. They are strategies to force the other person to love you, but this is impossible because true love can only be given freely. Even when we play this game very successfully and manage to win the attention of the other person, we know it was not spontaneous. We then no longer trust and we become insecure, frustrated and keep on creating new strategies.

The main feature of this vicious circle is the need for exclusive love. Having your expectations met and being loved is not enough. You must be loved exclusively. Everything has to be for you. The person who is with you cannot look away. He or she has to look at you 24 hours a day. In this case, how can you trust and relax? It is not possible to be in control all the time.

Note that this game is a great slavery. However, this slavery is created by the mind to sustain the false identity. It is the false self that believes in neediness. It believes itself to be a beggar and it keeps begging for attention. This creates what is, in fact, the greatest misery of the human being: affective neediness. This is an emotional illness that distorts the perception of reality. In this limited reality created by the ego, you depend on the approval, recognition and consideration of the other person. The philosopher Jean-Paul Sartre said: "Hell is other people." In this case, the other person becomes the reason for your anxiety, your sadness and your stress. But who is the other? Who is this other person you consider to be so important? Could it not be just a projection of the false self?

False success

As we have already seen, the ego plays an important role in the evolution of the human consciousness, since it is the ego that undertakes the journey. We need an ego to exist on this terrestrial plane and carry out our mission. It is our vehicle and also a mediator between the internal and external world. Through it, the soul can experience matter and express itself in the world. For its part, the ego is programmed based on a series of inputs related to what it needs to do in order to be important, successful and prosperous. What determines the ego's program is the need to have power and success to please and be recognized.

But what, at the end of the day, is success?

Real success means the realization of the purpose of the soul, but most people think it is the realization of the ego. As we have seen, the ego is programmed based on belief inherited from the outside world, and this program usually has no connection with the program of the soul. This means the person has often achieved success on an external level but still feels empty and frustrated. What happens is that the ego has become specialized in a certain thing, has learned to operate in the world and, by doing so, has gained material success. The person has become a specialist in *doing* but not in *being*. However, fulfillment is only achieved when the *being* and *doing* are aligned, and this alignment only occurs when the internal purpose (of the soul) also manifests itself externally.

Another way of looking at the ego is as if it were a character. It is dressed in a body and is the leading character of the story of our incarnation. It is this character who experiences human life, lives through situations and absorbs the lessons. We are not this character or this body. We are the spirit which is behind this guise, but the ego gains strength in the course of life and the character becomes incorporated in such a way that we start to believe we are the character.

This new identity with which we get identified creates a constant feeling of anguish and of being misplaced, which some people interpret as a feeling of emptiness. It is as though something is always missing. This creates the impression that something still needs to be done or conquered.

We are always dissatisfied and wanting more as nothing can fill the emptiness of not being who we are. But we are not aware of this for a certain time and end up building our whole life based on this forged identity. We achieve many things from this starting point. We can build real empires, win great success, fame, money and power but we cannot gain true happiness. There is nothing new in what I am saying. The old saying "money doesn't bring happiness" is just common sense, but the truth is that deep down we believe it does.

So we fight for money and, in this way, we even gain some joy but it is temporary, as fragile as a candle in the wind. This is a transient happiness that comes and goes in line with the movement of the season, in accordance with the latest fashion. You buy a new car and this makes you very happy until a new model is launched or your workmate buys a better car. You fall in love and are in ecstasy for a few months or weeks until you get to know the other person better and you start to see that he or she was not as perfect as you had thought. Your happiness only lasts as long as the other person matches your expectations. While he or she is at your side, looking only at you and giving you complete attention, you feel very important and confident, but it just needs a moment for the other one to glance aside and you start feeling miserable. If your happiness depends on someone else, if everything you have won is done so you appear important for the other person, then this is not happiness but dependence.

True happiness can only be born from what is real and permanent. And what is real stems from inner fulfilment. It is when we can feel complete in being what we are. This is only possible when we can display the purpose of our soul. This is true success. It is a feeling of satisfaction, fulfilment, being in the right place. When this happens, we are in harmony with the flow of life and our needs are met naturally. Everything improves, including the material life. When prosperity is the result of finding yourself, it is a divine gift that is at the service of the greater purpose. However, until we touch this internal core, everything we produce and build is done to escape from something or to protect us from something.

False wealth

We often frantically pursue material wealth to cover up the poverty within us. Sometimes *karma* allows this wealth to be built in the matter. However, if the wealth has no real solid base in truth, i.e. it does not result from the fulfilment of the soul but is, in fact, a product of the fear of scarcity, it will inevitably collapse. This kind of richness has no soul as it is not rooted in the heart. It may bring passing joy but does not create peace. The opposite in fact: it can become a burden. Many people win fortunes but are incapable of relaxing and enjoying them as they are always afraid of losing something. This is a wealth based on greed. Some people become slaves to the idea that they are only liked because of what they have, and this is true sometimes because these people were only concerned with *having* and not *being*.

This soulless wealth with no foundation in the heart must collapse at some point because everything that is built on a lie will inevitably have to be torn down. The essence of the human experience is the expansion of consciousness. That is why everything we build needs to have solid bases in the internal world. A sandcastle cannot remain standing when the tide comes in. It needs a solid, resistant foundation to stay upright, which means it needs to be true. To achieve this, we need to remove the defense mechanisms that are at the service of lie—the lie that you are needy of love. This can only be achieved through self-knowledge.

There is nothing wrong with wealth. The problem is the absence of oneself. What you have conquered outside is not a problem. The problem is in not conquering yourself.

Self-knowledge is the same as remembering yourself. When we remember our real identity, we automatically return to the path of the heart, which is the program of our soul. This is the match, the alignment I am talking about, because, by diverging from the path of the heart, we start feeling that we don't fit in. If we are not following the program of our soul, the size of the success we have conquered in the world does not matter. We continue to carry anguish. We often do not see this as we are so involved in the struggle for success or survival, but we are always anxious, down, sad . . . out of place.

Sometimes you have a glimmer of awareness and notice that something is wrong. You see that you might need to find another way in your life, but the mind is so burdened with information from outside, so contaminated by beliefs of what is right and wrong, that you become confused and lost. Despite this, you keep on going, dissatisfied, but without knowing where you are headed. You know there is something wrong but you still cannot identify what it is because apparently nothing seems to be out of place. You have a great home, a beautiful family, a big car in the garage, a stable job . . . There is no reason for dissatisfaction! Every time the anxiety knocks on your door, you pretend you do not see it and try to flee and run after the most varied distractions: the Internet, television, shopping . . . Symbolic needs are created to numb the pain behind this anxiety. These needs are transformed into addictions that work to numb consciousness through what you guard in the dungeons of your unconscious, the content that has been denied.

Numbing Devices

Let us get a better understanding of what I am calling "numbing device." This is a word I usually use to describe a process of internal anesthesia. Numbing is a way of removing something from our field of perception, a way of lowering awareness. It is a mechanism to escape from reality and is similar to the denial process I described earlier but acts on the human psyche at different times and depths.

Denial is when we are led to break with our true nature and is a way of anesthetizing the pain brought about by the break with our essence. The energy we use to anesthetize this original pain is our vital energy, the very substrata of pleasure. We use the very energy of pleasure to offset our suffering and, in doing so, create a link between pleasure and suffering. In other words, we start feeling pleasure in suffering and this is one of the reasons why suffering perpetuates itself on this planet.

Numbing involves the removal of the energy from the pleasure that a certain object or situation puts us in. The mechanism is the same but operates on a more superficial level, a layer over another. The numbing devices or buffers act to maintain those contents within the unconsciousness that were guarded there in childhood through denial. However, they are more easily identifiable through self-observation precisely because they form a more superficial layer.

Addictions are the most obvious numbing devices, but anything can become a numbing device. Any object, situation or thing we do may be used in this way. This will depend on our attitude towards life. Every situation gives us the chance of choosing whether we will use what life offers us to numb ourselves or as a wakeup call for consciousness. We always have the choice of cultivating suffering or taking advantage of the situation to grow and free ourselves from it. This choice depends on how mature we are and our willingness to grasp the reins of our own destiny.

There are various classes of numbing devices that have the task of anaesthetizing different aspects of the consciousness. Some are more dense and easier to identify, such as smoking and alcohol, for example. Others are more difficult as they are usually associated with something positive, such as compulsive doing and doing things without being present.

Doing something in a compulsive way has become a virtue in a world in which the race for success and competition has become normal behavior. The person who does not show this compulsion in this world is often regarded as lazy. However, compulsiveness, like laziness, may end up lulling consciousness to sleep. While laziness is a paralysis, an internal freeze that has the function of keeping feelings denied, compulsive doing is an excess of movement that is used to achieve the same result.

Doing things without being present is another aspect of compulsive doing. If you do not put your soul into what you are doing, this action becomes a pastime. It does not matter what the activity is. If you aren't fully present in each action, it will only be a distraction. In this sense, even self-knowledge and spiritual practice can be numbing devices. What should awaken consciousness becomes a way of soothing it to sleep. This happens when you repeat a mantra and carry out certain spiritual rituals in a mechanical way or when you develop the psychoanalytical addiction of analyzing everything. You think you are present, but this is a mechanical act, a habit. You think you are lucid, but the fact is that you are moving increasingly further from reality. You are desperately fleeing from it. You are a prisoner of mind games.

When I say "put the soul" into an action I mean that this action must be driven by a purpose—the soul's purpose. People are doing lots of things in the world, but none of these things are connected to their purpose. Doing things became compulsive precisely because this behavior is being used to numb existential anguish. This action has become a way of survival, a pastime until death arrives. Many people are in this situation as they have become used to it and it became a comfort zone. Some will pass their entire lives without remembering that, at one moment, they dreamt of achieving something. I am referring here to the dream as a revelation of the purpose of the soul, as a command from the higher Self. Some forget that they received this command one day and they simply start doing something in order to survive. Some people do something to feed the mask and crystalize the ego, to gain power. However, this action is compulsive and completely disconnected from the purpose of the soul. It is doing something without presence. Everything is done through the simple force of habit.

Regardless of its nature, desire is what upholds addictions and numbing devices. It is a bottomless well: the more we fulfill them, the more desires we have. This happens because desires are born from neediness, and neediness cannot be fulfilled from the outside in. It is an emotional state in which we believe we do not have what we need. What can free us from this state is the recognition that everything we are seeking so compulsively outside ourselves exists in abundance within us.

We saw earlier that we lost awareness of the source of life that inhabits us at some point on our journey. This source, which nurtures us and meets all of our needs, is within us, but we forgot this truth. This creates a deep sense that something is lacking, and that is neediness. Neediness turns us into beggars while we remain sitting on a chest of diamonds.

I generally use the chest as a metaphor for our internal wealth, as a symbol that represents this source from which everything we need comes. It is the field of pure potentiality, a place where everything is possible and where nothing is lacking.

Classic numbing devices

The main numbing mechanisms that prevent the awakening of consciousness are sex, money and food, but, obviously, these three elements are part of the human experience on Earth. In fact, they are also tools of development. However, as a result of the distortions, they have become numbing devices. A distortion occurs when the lower Self takes ownership over something. When fear and hate take over a legitimate instrument of development, it becomes toxic.

Food, sex and power are forces that were distorted and began being used to soothe the latent pains and anguish of the human being, which is why I usually call them "classic numbing devices." These three elements have an enormous power of putting consciousness to sleep.

Food – our social life revolves around food. Our daily routine is programmed according to our meals. Eating is one of the main forms of leisure for people and one of the few sources of pleasure for many people. It is interesting to note that, while many people starve, others suffer because they cannot stop eating as much as they do. Some live focused on the lack of food and others focus on the abundance of it. Few people understand the power food exercises in our lives, not only for the reasons I have just mentioned but also because it is our fuel. Our body is made by food and moved by the energy it brings. What we eat is transformed into our body and, in this sense, we are literally what we eat. Although science has recently managed to measure the influence of what we consume, even in terms of the genetic mutations, this dimension of human life is still a mystery to us.

Sex – one of humanity's greatest compulsions. You may even not have sex but you don't get it out of your mind. It is actually precisely due to repressing sexual desire that human beings have become dependent on pornography and the distortions of sexuality. I usually say that lust is the queen of this world, but when I speak of lust I am not making a moral judgment but actually referring to the use of sexual energy to manipulate, dominate and obtain power over the other. There is nothing wrong with sex. It is natural. The problem lies in the sexual distortions and perversions. They are the great drug.

Power – our greatest addiction is the desire for power, particularly in the form of money. We all basically agree that the human being is totally dependent on money. If lust is the queen of this world, then money is the king. Money is synonymous with power. You can buy what you want with it, and this may include individuals. People live to earn money while they should be earning money to live. They have a lot to spend but do not have the time to do so. Money has become the means and the end in itself. Many believe that, besides money, success also means having an important position, influence over lots of people or being famous.

Understanding numbing devices* is essential if we are to be aware of what keeps us far from the truth. However, it is also important to understand that I am not judging or criticizing the use of these numbing tools. I understand that the pain is sometimes so acute that you cannot cope with it. When a headache is very strong, we normally have to take a painkiller, but, if the pain persists, it is necessary to look for the cause. The same happens on the emotional level: you use a certain resource to numb the pain until you can build a solid emotional structure that can hold it. But why is the contact with the pain important? Because this core of pain contains the cause of the illness and, therefore, the cure. The problem is when you become addicted to the painkiller and do not want to stop using it. As a result, you shut off access to the core of the pain and prevent the possibility of a cure. Under the effect of the anesthetics, you think everything is all right and "normal". You are not feeling the pain and, as a result, you think you are healthy, but the fact is that you are becoming sicker and sicker.

Addiction, regardless of the kind, is a numbing device that serves to protect attachments. It is not important what kind of addiction you have. By becoming an addict, you are protecting yourself and, at the same time, fleeing from something. Deep down you are running away from yourself. For some reason, there is fear of looking inside yourself and seeing the reality. Maybe you are ashamed of something. Maybe you are afraid of seeing that your whole life has been built on a fantasy, a fiction.

---

* See **Key Practice 4**: Identifying and removing numbing devices (p. 126).

The fact is that you created a story at some time in your life and started living in it in order to be able to deal with the pain. This was the way you found to alleviate the pain of being repressed, humiliated, forgotten, abandoned, rejected . . . It was then you became the main character in this story and started to believe that you were this character. With the passing of time, you clung to the elements of the narrative you created.

Most stories have at least three characters: a hero, a villain and a victim, and you switch between these different roles, depending on the stage of your life. Some people spend their whole lives in a single role because the numbing device is efficient in this case. However, in most cases, the numbing device gradually loses force and you need to change the character. There is always a need for change but being attached to the role makes you feel constantly threatened. You are always afraid and the fear is proportional to the extent of your attachment. When life invites you to make a change, it is seen as a danger. But what is the danger? The biggest danger is to discover that the story you have always believed was your life is only an invention of the mind.

The numbing devices are used to anaesthetize and remove the fear at the same time. However, you are afraid of losing your conquests precisely because they are your anesthetics. Your wounds are still open because, as you are in no condition to deal with them, you had to deny them. You do not notice this internal process because of the anesthesia but the pains of the past are there, influencing your present life. If you are unaware of this, your life is being driven by the past and your current choices are influenced by it.

Normosis

Somebody once said to me, "Okay, I'm really hooked. I'm addicted to sex, alcohol, pornography . . . but if everything is going well in my life, why do I have to change anything? Why do I have to track down the pain? Why can't I continue like this?"

One of the most common symptoms of the deep numbness in which human beings find themselves is normosis. This is a psychological illness, the main symptom of which is an almost hypnotic state in which the person believes everything is completely "normal": corruption is normal, violence is normal, telling a "little lie" is normal; betrayal is normal, competition, pretending, cheating, traffic jams . . . Everything is normal. Your relationships are pointless and never last more than a few weeks but this is normal; you spend more time on the Internet looking for pictures of women than with your own partner, but this is normal; you cannot feel joy at a party without drinking alcohol but this is normal; the planet is being destroyed, the animals are being killed, the garbage we produce is being sent into space, our food is contaminated . . . but everything in your life is okay because everything is normal!

So the answer is "yes, you can continue to live like this." You can choose to live for some time in an anaesthetized state, at least until the moment when *karma* knocks on your door, i.e. until the effect of your actions begins to appear in your life. This effect can emerge in various ways: in the form of a loss, an illness, a frustration, an accident, or even as a passion. Life is movement and everything is in a constant state of transformation. There is a time when life brings a challenge that makes you want to get moving.

You will probably manage to lead your life with a certain degree of numbing for some time (some people even do so throughout their whole existence) until something important happens that brings a surprise and you get a shock. You start to feel uncomfortable. You start to feel an anguish, a worry without any explanation. Questions then start arising about the meaning of life. You notice that you are not happy despite everything being "normal", despite everything being "well." The older you become, the sadder you feel because you know you have conquered many things but you have still not conquered yourself. When this worry knocks on your door, you ask yourself, "What have I done with my life? I built houses, bought things, became cultured, but I still don't know who I am. I don't know why I'm here."

3. Death of the False Self

HOLY CRISIS

The time comes when the numbing devices are no longer efficient, just like a drug that creates tolerance and demands a higher and higher intake in order to offer the desired effect. In this case, the side effects begin to become unbearable, and the risk of an overdose becomes imminent. We often need to reach this level of suffering so that, through a vital impulse, we find the forces needed for the transformation.

When someone gets to this point, one sees that there is only a single choice available: he or she must change or die. Because even if the person is not addicted to a chemical drug, he or she is addicted to something that has become poisonous and is slowly dying. This could be a life situation that does not correspond to the soul's wish, which means that the person is moving in the opposite direction from his or her purpose. That is when the chance to see reality and make a choice comes. When I talk about death, in this case, it is in the sense of living without joy or pleasure—this is the same as dying. One often needs to reach this stage so a change of direction that can transform his or her life can occur.

Unfortunately, this is how things work, with suffering being what usually creates the impulse for transformation. Change normally arrives through a great existential void, depression, a great loss or an illness. When I say this, I do not mean that we have to suffer to evolve, but it is a fact that this is what has been happening throughout the history of humanity. I have been working so that we can be driven by love, and not by suffering but this will only be possible through a change of culture.

Collapse of what is false

The moment comes when everything begins to collapse. And the fall is in proportion to the size of the building. The greater the empire constructed by the ego, the greater the crash. The greater the material conquest, the greater the comparison between what was gained outside and what was not achieved internally. If there is an empire outside but nothing inside you, you become desperate. You may become aware that everything you have done and all your victories have served to achieve absolutely nothing as, at the last moment, you will not even take a grain of dust with you. The only thing you take is your own self. The only thing that really makes sense and can be achieved is yourself—your true identity.

When you are a stranger to yourself, not even the whole world can fulfill you. You wake in the morning and ask yourself: "What for?" You get dressed and set off in life, but you are always questioning yourself. Nothing makes sense, nothing brings satisfaction. And nothing the world offers is enough. You feel dissatisfied and frustrated and often depressed. Life becomes a burden. The things you regarded as normal suddenly become absurd because you are starting to see the senselessness of the way in which you live and of your relationship with the world.

I am not saying that it is wrong to gain assets or become rich. Prosperity is also a divine manifestation. I am referring to the fact that many people waste their lives in a frantic search for material wealth. They waste their lives looking for happiness by accumulating things. This is insane.

A sensible man is the one who looks for happiness within himself. Nevertheless, regardless of the wealth the person might have acquired or the poverty in which the person is living, this existential crisis is an emergency: something needs to change! This is a profound crisis, but it is absolutely essential as it is what makes you move towards transformation.

I have said that, deep down, crises are positive. This can be seen not only in the personal but also in the collective sphere. It does not matter if it is a political, economic, financial or environmental crisis. It does not matter if it is cancer, a stomach ache or acne . . . If there is a crisis now, it is because something had already gone wrong a long time before it showed itself. Until the time the crisis emerges, everything seems to be good, everything looks "normal." Until the symptoms arise, you appear to be healthy, but the truth is that the illness (which is also a kind of crisis) was already in the process of being established in your system for a long time. Therefore, the crisis is only an outbreak, the exhibition of something that was submerged but was strengthened by bad habits, conditioning and behavior that were contaminated by fear.

From this angle, the crisis is a blessing because if we examine what is behind the symptoms, we will have the chance to recognize and treat the illness at its origin. Therefore, it is an opportunity for healing and growth.

Suppressed love

I cannot pass over this topic without touching on the question of depression as I believe we are facing a real epidemic of this disturbance. As I mentioned earlier, depression has become the illness of the century, and this reflects the point we have reached in the evolutionary journey. Even if we have made great advances in scientific discoveries, we have not yet found a solution for this kind of imbalance. The opposite in fact: suicide rates are scary. We have created machines that can go beyond the Earth's atmosphere and visit other planets, but we still do not have technologies that are efficient enough to transcend neediness and cure the obsession for power. We still haven't been able to find solutions for our environmental problems, nor for the high indices of poverty and violence in the world. I often joke about how great it would be if we could create a pill to awaken love. This would be the pill that cures all illnesses since love is the universal solvent for all evils.

Depression is a symptom of suppressed love, of love stored away in a safe. In other words, it is a symptom of a closed heart. This closure, this blockage of energy, really changes the chemistry of the brain. Love is the very sap of life. It makes everything grow and prosper. If love is not circulating in the system then the levels of dopamine and serotonin, among other hormones, will become low and, therefore, you will get physically depressed. This state will make it increasingly more difficult for you to open your heart and even for you to seek ways to solve the problem. It is another vicious circle.

Sometimes it is necessary to use medication to interrupt this circle and to reorganize the chemistry of the brain, but most of the drugs used create dependency, which actually worsens the situation. Chemical intervention can help to ease the symptoms initially, but it is important not to lose the path to the cure. It is important to remember that the chemical disorganization of the system is only a symptom and not the cause.

The cause is the love that is blocked. In order to unblock it, a certain amount of courage is needed. Courage to break with the mechanical approach, i.e. the conditioning that prevents you from seeing life from another angle.

Often everything seems to be going very well in your material life, but you remain dissatisfied and depressed. For as organized as your life may be, you feel that something is out of place, although you can't tell what it is. Sometimes it is difficult to recognize it, but there is always a clue. In this case, I suggest you ask yourself: "If I did not have to earn money or please someone, what would I do with my life? What would I do with my time?"

This is a good question that could mark the beginning of a healing process. If you let yourself go deep into this study, you will be able to see that you are not allowing your soul to show what it wants. You are not letting love pass. To put it another way, you are not allowing yourself to be spontaneous because you are imprisoned in a social role.

Ask yourself: "Who is playing this role? Who is the character in this story?"

I always say and I repeat it here that you need courage to change because you often enter a comfort zone with this character. What happens is that the personality has been trained since an early age to do what is right, according to society's standards. This is necessary to a certain extent but you cease being a child and become an adult who is imprisoned within these limits. You grow up physically, but you remain at the same point emotionally. You then do what is right (according to the social standards) to receive love and attention, but this prevents you from being spontaneous and natural. When you condemn spontaneity, you also condemn your mental health. And one of the main symptoms of this repression of your spontaneity is precisely depression.

One common aspect of all depressive syndromes is the feeling of loneliness, of being apart and, in turn, unprotected. The person usually isolates himself or herself and stops relating to the world. They can even achieve success in certain areas of life, which brings relief and hides the symptoms of depression for a while. The symptoms sometimes appear when the person is alone and, on waking up in the middle of the night, feels despair, or even when they do not want to get up in the morning. There are occasions when foggy feelings and panic attacks occur, but there is always a feeling of detachment, a lack of meaning in life, a sadness with no apparent cause. The person cannot explain why he or she is sad but continues to get on with their life automatically. The person is not there. The soul is not present because it feels imprisoned and cannot expand. Perhaps the best statement to sum up the state of depression is to say that "life is suffering."

I see that, regardless of the personal imprints that we carry, we are also passing through a zone of depression on a collective level. When I say collective, I am referring to humanity, to the human race. The world is passing through a grey zone. This is happening because consciousness is expanding and we are beginning to see this great disconnection that has led us to the highest level of environmental and spiritual degradation, as well as degradation of human values. We are beginning to become aware of our insanity to a certain extent.

Enduring pain

I have come to the conclusion that one of the main challenges of the human journey is to feel, or even better, deal with what we feel. I see that only the willingness to face up to the existential pains that inhabit us can cure humanity since it is these pains that create our insanity. Is it not insane to kill each other? Is it not insane to destroy our planet? Is it not insane to pollute rivers? Is it not insane to pollute the Earth? Is it not insane to destroy our source of life? For me, all of this is insane, but it is an insanity brought about by the unconscious pain that we carry.

It is so challenging to experience and deal with feelings that we end up putting ourselves within an armor. We create a wall between ourselves and the world and become insensitive because this wall does not allow us to feel. We do this because, at some level, there is an idea that feeling is very dangerous. This idea exists because of a memory we carry. As we have already seen, at some point in our life we have had painful experiences that are difficult to bear and, as a result, we need to numb the pain. So we erect a wall that is built with many feelings: pride, fear, revenge, hate, rationalizing and various other defense mechanisms. However, if we are to move ahead in this journey, this wall will have to be destroyed. At some time, we will have to take off the armor and become vulnerable. It is only by doing so that we will be able to learn how to deal with the feelings.

This learning is a necessary passage in the evolutionary process, also because you can only sustain ecstasy if you manage to withstand sadness, as the channel of feeling is the same.

Both sadness and ecstasy pass through the same channel. Therefore, by suppressing feelings in order not to feel pain, you are also making it impossible to feel pleasure.

Someone once said that emotions are like wild horses. They are untamable, and feelings are like rapids that you cannot control and do not know where they will take you. However, you have to deal with this at some point. You will need to learn to confront the vulnerability and uncertainty that feelings bring. Just as the feelings can lead you to the depths of the unconsciousness and trigger great fear, despair and anguish that cannot be translated into words, they can also take you to marvelous experiences and make you cry out of joy and gratitude.

Dealing with feelings that have been denied is an inevitable passage. If you have built a well-founded wall, this means there are existential pains so deeply rooted that they make you afraid of feeling the pain of annihilation. Some feelings are really mortifying, but this wall will have to be toppled and this will only happen when you are willing to investigate, when you consciously decide to see what is behind it.

You need to show humility and courage to confront the pain and deal with the denied feelings. You need the humility to admit that things were really not easy but do this without exaggerating the extent of the pain, i.e. without fantasizing and falling into the trap of claiming to be a victim. It is also necessary to have humility to recognize that the rose has thorns. Courage is needed to face up to these pains, and this means facing up to the thorn and removing it. However, removing the thorn causes pain, particularly if it is embedded in the flesh. The fact that you are used to it does not mean it does not hurt. On the contrary: it must be infected, creating gangrene that you do not feel as you are numb. Therefore, tackling the thorn will hurt more at first than when it was thrust into your flesh.

Looking at the thorns means coming into contact with memories and traumas that you always wanted to forget. To want to forget or wish something did not exist is not enough. You want to be free of the past, but it remains there. You can only free yourself from the past when you come to terms with it.

Identifying our disturbances, worries and madness is the first step. However, the path between identifying the illness and reaching the cure is often long. That is why it is necessary to be committed to the cure. This is really valuable. It is rare to meet people in this world who have this lucidity.

Therefore, to be yourself, you not only need humility but also commitment, courage and steadiness to free yourself from the defenses, tear down the walls and take off the armor and masks. You will need to become vulnerable to do so. You can only show the purpose of the soul by being disarmed. This is why I say that identifying that you are defending yourself, that you are fighting and that you are armed is a measure of success. It is only through the process of becoming aware of this that you have the power to awaken yourself. When you notice something you had not noticed before, it means your consciousness is already expanding.

That is why I have been saying that humanity's great conquest has nothing to do with scientific advances but, in fact, with the ability to identify what was denied and learn to deal with the dark nature. The ability to treat the pain. Even with all the technology we have developed and the money we have accumulated, we have still not learnt to cope with anger, jealousy, envy, frustration . . . Therefore, I think it is really valuable for the human being to learn how to face up to these contents, i.e. the existential pains that inhabit us. Our inability to cope with this means we simply remove these feelings from our field of view, numb ourselves, and create masks.

This does not mean I am against technological and scientific advances. Very much the opposite. I am a user and researcher of new solutions providing they are aligned with the sustainable development of the human being and serve the higher purpose. We have certainly made many technological breakthroughs over the last three decades. There has never been so much money in the world. However, we continue to kill each other. There is nothing wrong with technology and the marvels of architecture, art, and engineering. There is nothing wrong with money. The question is how we have been using it.

I see that humanity has become stuck at this point of the study: it needs to learn and grow through suffering but it is unable to deal with the pain. This paradox has created unnecessary suffering, which is why I say that if there is something of real value in this world, it is self-knowledge. This is the path.

4. Rebirth

TURNING WITHIN

I have received many people of all kinds who face an existential crisis and are trying to find another direction. Some are highly successful. Others have gained fame, power and lots of money. In terms of material and social wealth, they have won everything a human being would like and can conquer in this world, yet they still feel empty and dissatisfied. I receive all of them—regardless of their life stories, honoring their attitude, as it takes lots of courage and willingness to face up to the truth. There must be a willingness to go within yourself just as there has to be a willingness to move outside.

If you are in a state where nothing satisfies you or you are frustrated enough with the world (as Siddhartha Gautama, the Buddha, became frustrated with his palace and all his wealth) you are close to a big change. It is only when you are tired of the world that you can move on from the unreal to the real since lots of courage and willingness is needed to close your eyes and switch off from the outside world.

The journey is an internal one. When I say that the real is born from fulfillment, I mean that this happens when we actually find this point within ourselves, i.e. when the purpose of the soul (internal) shows itself externally. Until we touch this core within us, everything we produce is directed at fleeing or protecting ourselves from something.

Commands of the heart

Those who are, to some extent, shaken and start to question the meaning of life begin to turn within. Having been really touched by the Mystery of life, the essence of which is the constant transformation and expansion of consciousness, you feel impelled to move towards it. It is as though you had heard a mysterious call that leads you to look for something greater, something that is beyond material realization. When this happens, a long journey of self-knowledge starts, leading you to meet your true identity once again and, in turn, to the revelation of your purpose.

However, many people go through life without hearing this internal call, which is always inviting you to follow the path of the heart. The fact is that most people are totally deaf and unable to hear the commands of the heart. They are hypnotized and anaesthetized, pursuing money and power, concentrating mainly on living a life that the conditioned mind believes is good.

Many of those who could hear the call will not have the courage to heed it. Some seekers of truth are already on the path but do not have the courage to change. They want to have an experience of what is real but are not willing to give up small habits; they do not have the willingness to give up an addiction. They desire realization, but besides not pursuing self-knowledge, they are afraid of the transformation that is needed for it to come about. Life then passes and they continue to only dream about this. However, realization is not possible on the dream level. Realization is synonymous with awakening, which means to stop dreaming.

Deep down, we are talking about a move from fear to trust. Fear ties us down to a certain place and creates a sense of security, but we pay a very high price for this security. We pay with our joy and our life. Many people will be unable to follow the commands of the heart as they prefer to maintain this false idea of security.

Following the heart involves risks, as certain things are obviously in play. This depends on how you have chosen to structure your life. For example, if you have a family, some laws will have to be respected. Some will need to make the sacrifice of renouncing an internal command to comply with certain agreements made during the incarnation. In this case, they will prefer even not to know what the heart says.

Self-knowledge can be a great danger for these people. This is because, when you know yourself, you will inevitably come into contact with your dissatisfactions and fears which creates an impulse for change. But it is much easier and, apparently, safer to leave everything as it is than to have to dismantle a system that is already structured in place. It is more comfortable to live the familiar lifestyle, waiting for death to arrive, than make a move towards something new. However, what they do not know is that a treasure lies behind this command of the heart, waiting for us. Self-knowledge is the treasure map. The worst thing is that many of those who know this give up the treasure, even though they have an idea of what lies within it. At the deepest level, this treasure represents the presents we have to deliver to the world and is a symbol of what we have come to do here, a symbol of the goal of the soul.

Wisdom of uncertainty

To achieve the goal, i.e. the soul's purpose, you need to be willing to navigate the wisdom of uncertainty. This means learning to listen and follow the commands of the heart, even without knowing where the heart wants to take you. You act and surrender the result of your action to the Mystery. You renounce expectations in relation to the outcome of situations. In this way, life becomes a great adventure, an experience in which the conditioned mind will unavoidably be deconstructed. Nothing is certain in this adventure—anything can happen.

By allowing yourself to enter this adventure, you open yourself up to the field of pure potentiality, a space where anything is possible. You allow yourself to be in this place where everything you need manifests itself, since you are entering into contact with the source of abundance and of power that inhabits you. I am referring here to the real power, that which is born from the fulfillment of your Being and not from the ego's neediness. By permitting yourself to have trust in the wisdom of uncertainty you enter this space in which we are one with the Mystery; this place of Unity in which your needs are naturally provided by the universe.

I know this might sound more like a fairy tale than reality to lots of people because they are a long way from allowing themselves to live an experience like this. For those who still strongly identify with the fear of scarcity, this transition from fear to trust may be almost impossible, but the only way of knowing whether it is possible is to try and run the risk.

You can choose to make a smooth transition. If you program yourself to do so, this can bring some comfort as it is not always possible to simply leave everything behind and follow the command. If you have commitments and agreements to be met, it would not be wise to abandon them. The heart will always lead you to act with wisdom and compassion. If you feel the need to make a move, but this could leave some accounts open, then pay attention to the chance that it is not the voice of your heart, but the conditioned mind that is speaking. The heart is leading you to the realization of your purpose, your goal, your greatest dream. To achieve this, you will need to free yourself from unfinished business.

The heart speaks through synchronicities, the mysterious signs or apparent coincidences you cannot explain. But the mental conditioning is sometimes so deep that you cannot understand the signs. You have unlearned the language of the heart and are no longer able to understand what it says. In this case, you may need some time to allow yourself not to make any decision, a breathing space in which you can relax and relearn the language of the signs from your heart.

Trap of doubt

Let us imagine that you have heard a command, paid attention to the signs of life and decided to follow a certain path. At that moment, you felt the whole universe was on your side because everything began to happen in a fluid, easy and effortless way. You were then certain that this was the right path. However, something happens in the middle of this route. An accident or something that leaves you shaken. At that moment you wonder: have I chosen the wrong road? Not necessarily. When you follow the path of the heart, some obstacles and challenges will naturally arise, but this does not mean your choice was wrong. The proof of this lies exactly in the fact that the whole universe came together in your favor at the beginning.

As I have just said, you need to be free of open accounts, at least to a certain point, in order to fulfill the purpose of your soul. If the heart sometimes takes us to the right and other times to the left, it is because there is some learning for us. There is something in that place to be integrated, understood and cured. The heart guides us along a certain road precisely so that the purifications that are needed happen and we can be ready for the realization of the greater goal. However, this process of liberation can be quite unpleasant, so you rebel, you shut down and fall into the trap of doubt.

What happens is that you need to bring together all the available forces in order to have courage to follow an unknown route. You need all the trust and willingness to go beyond fear. If you are really ready, the universe will help at this moment for you to take the first step and you will experience an illuminating moment in which everything flows in the most perfect way possible. This will go on until a purification process begins and, once again, you will feel insecure, confused and lost. Everything seems to be wrong and you are overwhelmed by a profound skepticism. You close yourself off at this moment until you can mature enough to understand that this situation that caused doubt and suffering is part of the purification. When you reach this understanding, you feel the whole universe is on your side. You feel blessed and everything flows once again. This process brings you a little closer to the chest of diamonds, but a new challenge soon appears.

That is how life is. The darkest moment of the night is just before dawn. The coldest moment of the night is just before sunrise. That is how this plane operates. But this is all part of a loving conspiracy of the universe to strengthen your trust and willpower.

I now recall the time in which I went out very early to meditate and wait for the sun to rise. Then the cold and a cloud of mosquitoes would arrive in force and all I wanted to do was to get up and run away from there. But I insisted on staying until the splendor of the sunrise appeared and sent the cold and mosquitoes away. It was worth it!

Renunciation or refuge

Another example that gives a good description of the ups and downs of the process within the path of the heart is when you undergo a deep existential crisis and, as a result, are motivated to surrender yourself to the spiritual life. You see that your lifestyle no longer makes sense, and you decide to leave everything behind and go and live in a spiritual community, an *ashram*.

When you arrive at this place, which is dedicated to the spirit, you feel the light, love and peace that pulsate there. You feel you have found your place. You then begin dedicating yourself to the spiritual practices, feel at peace, you feel that you are in the right place and even decide to become celibate. However, as time passes, the relationship challenges begin to emerge and you begin to want to do other things. This leads you to an internal conflict. You thought you were ready to renounce the world but still have desires and find it difficult to relate in a constructive way.

The *ashram* is, above all, a house of Truth. This means it is the kind of place where you will have to come into contact with the Truth at some time or other. If you are in this place to escape from something, the reason why you are fleeing will appear sooner or later in an even stronger way because everything becomes more defined in this place—black becomes blacker and white becomes whiter.

What I mean by this is that it does not matter what you are fleeing from as you will only free yourself from this when you can face it. You can only free yourself of your internal ghosts if you can face them, because the more you run away, the more they run after you. They start appearing where you least expect them. Wherever you are, whether in the office working or in the *ashram* praying, you will have to deal with these ghosts that prevent you from relating in a constructive way. You will inevitably have to overcome the difficulty you have to remain present while you relate. You will inevitably have to overcome your fears. And to learn this, you may have to return to the world.

It does not matter what you are doing but how you are doing it. What matters is that the action must be driven by the heart and be carried out with presence, with the soul. Doing something with the soul means being aware of the purpose of the action. By acting from presence, even knowing that your place is the *ashram*, you understand that your soul is leading you back to the world to close open accounts. If you are aware of the purpose of your soul then, no matter where you are, any place is the ideal space for its fulfillment.

However, if you are at the stage of affirmation of the ego, i.e. if your ego still needs to grow and build things in the world, do not worry so much about surrendering. Focus on fulfilling your desires and conquering what you need. Go after the money you think you need to earn and the fame you need to have. Everything is all right! Don't fall into the trap of the spiritual ego that believes that what is right is to give all this up. You can only give up what you have. Therefore, don't fool yourself.

5. Maturity

GIFTS AND TALENTS

The purpose is the mission, the soul's program within the incarnation. There is an individual and a collective purpose and both are related: the collective purpose can only be fulfilled through each one of us. The purpose reveals itself in a particular way in each of our lives, depending on the different gifts the soul brings and the learning it needs to absorb. However, only one purpose exists at the end of the day and that is the greater purpose that is our mission to humanity. Therefore, the individual purpose serves the greater purpose.

As we have seen, the ego also has a program, which I am calling the "external program" as it is created based on outside references (culture, education, family, amongst other social factors). The ego program often has no relation to the internal program, which is the soul's purpose. This contradiction has caused most of the existential crises the human being faces.

In dealing with this issue in my lectures, I notice that many people confuse what the purpose is with what the skills or gifts through which the purpose manifests itself are. The internal purpose is related to what the person does in the world but doing it in itself is not the purpose. What is being done is a tool through which purpose is realized.

Recognizing potentials

Every human being is born with certain abilities or latent potentials, which we can also call gifts. When a gift is developed, it becomes a talent, i.e. something the person does very well and easily. A person's talent is usually something he or she loves to do and is a passion.

I see many young people suffer with the difficulty to choose their life's profession. This difficulty exists because they have been unable to recognize their own gifts* and do not know what they really like to do. This is another symptom that stems from the mental conditioning created by a system that is obsessed with money. We live in an ambitious society that values financial power more than personal realization. Our education system does not provide the child with what they need to make contact with what he or she really likes. On the contrary, we are forced to study subjects and learn things in which we have no interest or aptitude and which, in most cases, will be of no use in our life. We are also led to believe that certain activities are better than others because they raise the social status and, in theory, ensure financial stability. The profession is often chosen according to market trends, and we end up turning our passions into weekend hobbies practiced erratically.

The media and social networks also exercise a great influence on our choices. They worship personalities, attitudes and lifestyles. Characters become models for behavior and people become idols. Advertising creates desires and stokes consumerism. In other words, the media

---

* See **Key Practice 5**: Recognizing potentials (p. 127).

encourages the desire for power and greed. It feeds the false Self and everything that empowers the ego. The ego is very ambitious and always dreams of grandiose things and has the fantasy that it came to do something very important and special or that, at some moment, it will become rich and famous. This often happens but it remains a mere fantasy in most cases and prevents the person from having access to what he or she really came here to do. Based on a mental image, the individual idealizes a lifestyle and ends up losing a lot of time trying to achieve something that has nothing to do with what he or she really came to achieve.

For example, let us assume that the ego wants to be a great spiritual leader or a famous artist but the soul's program is to live in a spiritual community and do *seva* (selfless service). The soul came to sweep up the room, clean the windows, cook for lots of people, water flowers, chant mantras, pray and meditate. Imagine the contradiction. A very ambitious person whose dream is fame and power but whose real life has drawn up paths that are completely the opposite will become anxious and anguished, to say the least. This individual often carries anguish and, depending on the scale of the inner conflict, will commonly manifest depression or even other physical and mental illnesses. This happens because these people are being torn apart internally: one force is pulling them in one direction and another force is pulling them in the other. The ego feeds great expectations, but the soul is not so ambitious.

Therefore, we are not encouraged to recognize, value and develop our true gifts that we are born with. This makes it impossible to fulfill the program of our soul. A gift needs to be tended if it is to grow. We can say we plant gifts to harvest talents. If a plant is to grow and give flowers and fruits, it needs water and light as well as fertile soil. Similarly, our gifts need to be fed, and this is done through dedication. Some gifts are so natural they do not require any effort to grow, while others need a certain dedication and willpower. Some gifts appear early in life, while others only appear with maturity. This is because certain gifts will only serve for the realization of the external program and, for this reason, they will be developed during the period of affirmation of the ego, which is when the individual dedicates himself or herself exclusively to personal development and material success. So, with the passing of time, when the ego has become sufficiently crystalized and the person starts learning that there must be a greater reason for being incarnated here, new skills start being revealed and developed.

Some people will not undergo this process because the ego program is already related to the soul's program, in some way. These individuals will continue to manifest the same talents throughout their entire lives. What changes in these cases is that, at some point, their action gains a new quality—it gains soul. The action that was previously carried out in an automatic and superficial way, only to match the external expectations, takes on a new meaning. Despite the talent and passion involved in the action, it was still at the service of the ego and neediness. Therefore, the time arrives when the action is given a new meaning and starts serving the higher purpose. In other words, *karma* aligns with *dharma* and something within fits.

Being and doing

When this fit occurs—the alignment between the external and internal purposes—we are taken by a deep feeling of fullness and belonging. It is as though we have finally returned home after traveling for many years. This is because a mismatch occurred between what we are and what we do when we broke with our essence and built a false identity. We have let a fictitious character take care of our home and started doing things that pleased others and added value to this false idea of Self. For this reason, this fit is the same as meeting yourself once again.

From this re-encounter, which is a source of great joy, the truth of who we are begins to appear through our actions. This is because what we do is intimately related to what we are. In fact, *being* and *doing* are as inseparable as a rose is from its perfume. Our gifts and talents are fragrances from the supreme Being who inhabits us, perfumes that are sprinkled in different actions in the world. They are the various qualities of our primordial essence: love.

So, one important point that needs to be understood is that the soul's purpose is not what we do but, in fact, who we are. The question of identity is essential in the process of unveiling the purpose of the soul. As we free ourselves from the false identity and activate the memory of who we really are, our purpose also reveals itself. When you ask yourself: "What did I come here to do?" you are also asking yourself: "Who am I?"

There is no doubt that our activities are related to our purpose, but, deep down, the purpose is the realization of what we are, i.e. self-realization. However, this self-realization does not relate to a professional or material achievement but actually to the memory of who we are.

When we awaken this memory, our soul's program will inevitably reveal itself, and our gifts and talents will become the means of expressing the truth about who we are. As a result, we become channels for the realization of the greater purpose. That is why I usually say that our gifts and talents are the presents we have brought to give to the world.

Kept Gifts

When this alignment occurs between the internal and external, between *dharma* and *karma*, between *being* and *doing*, we feel joy in waking in the morning to put our gifts and talents at the service of the greater good because, if our actions are aligned with the soul's purpose, they are naturally serving the greater purpose. We then feel a great comfort in being where we are and doing what we are doing.

However, many people still cannot have this experience as they are not aware of their gifts and are even less aware of the soul's purpose. Many others are actually aware of their gifts but, for some reason, refuse to put them into practice.

Whenever I talk about this subject, I recall a story that touches me a lot because of its symbolic richness. It is a Biblical passage that refers to some of the obstacles the seeker confronts during the process of awakening consciousness, which is the path to self-realization.

Jonah was an ardent seeker of truth and used to hear the voice of God talking to him. God once said to him: "Jonah, go to Nineveh. I want to save the people there and do so through you. I will speak through you to save those people."

However, Jonah did not like the command at all and decided to take a boat that was going in exactly the opposite direction. He went into the hold of the boat and fell into a deep sleep. Then God sent a ferocious storm and the boat began rocking from side to side. Everyone began to despair at the risk of imminent death. Then someone found Jonah, woke him up and said: "How can you sleep at a time like this?"

At that time, people used to throw dice to interpret the divine and communicate with the spiritual plane. So they played dice and discovered that the storm was happening because there was a stranger on the boat. They immediately concluded the stranger was Jonah and threw him overboard. At that moment, the storm ceased and Jonah was swallowed up by a sea monster. When he was inside the monster's mouth, he remembered to pray to God. That was when he heard the voice saying once again: "Jonah, go to Nineveh."

Why did Jonah not want to go to Nineveh? Because he kept wounds and resentment towards the people from there. He did not want those people to be saved. He was imprisoned by vengeance.

When you refuse to follow the path of the heart and refuse to put your gifts and talents in motion, this means you are sleeping, that you are heavily numb. Then God sends a ferocious storm that rocks everything around you and you say: "I don't feel anything. I have nothing to do with this." Everything seems to be going very well and is totally normal because you are completely numb. You continue in this state until something happens. You are swallowed up by a monster and enter a place where you are about to be crushed. The mouth of the monster represents a place of intense purification. And it is only when you receive a shock of this size that you start feeling again and seeing that everything that is happening is to help you give up your feelings of hurt, resentment and revenge. Everything is done for you to learn to surrender to the flow of life, which is always leading you to the realization of your purpose.

As long as you keep wounds and resentments in the form of pacts of vengeance (which means you have made no progress in the process of purification of the lower nature that lives within you), you will be unable to give your presents to the world. You may even hand over something but not everything. Being imprisoned in a vengeance pact* means you cannot give your best. You often refuse to offer your presents because you are afraid of your own greatness and of success. This seems absurd, but it is very common.

The fear of greatness or your revealed potential is the unfolding of another fear: that of doing better than your parents. Some people maintain co-dependent relationships with their parents, and these relationships show themselves through a feeling of powerlessness when faced with them.

These people unconsciously do not want to develop because they believe that by manifesting their gifts, they will do better than their parents and destroy the co-dependent relationship. Some people still manage to develop themselves but maintain a certain subservience because they feel guilty for being in a better place than their parents. Some suffer from this guilt to such an extent that they need to live far from their parents in order to prosper as they are incapable of breaking away from the misery of their family and ancestry.

---

* See **Key Practice 2:** Freeing trapped feelings and pacts of vengeance (p. 118).

This is one aspect of the inferior nature that is difficult to understand. It is a way of maintaining the vicious circles of suffering and occurs, unfortunately, because the human being has become used to suffering. This is the result of centuries and centuries of ignorance about life's higher purpose and lack of awareness of our own lower nature. We have learnt to defend ourselves by accusing other people. We do not know our own evil and thus we keep looking for others to blame for our own miseries. And the way we found to survive in the midst of such misery is to feel pleasure in suffering.

This is why I insist on the importance of self-knowledge. We need to be aware of our own evil. We need to know the dark corners of the mind, which are the shadowy aspects of the personality, if we are to be able to purify them from our system. The purification of the lower nature is the stage of the self-knowledge process in which we devote ourselves to the exploration of consciousness to identify those parts of us that, for some reason, we do not accept and that we hide and which act in spite of our conscious will, thereby sabotaging our happiness. If we do not develop ourselves sufficiently in this process, we cannot be truly happy and prosperous.

When you hand over the presents you brought to share and are happy with what you do, you become a link in the chain of happiness and prosperity—happiness and prosperity pass through you to reach others. When your gifts and talents are put into motion, this means that love is acting through you. And this naturally generates more happiness and prosperity, creating a benign circle.

However, there are some people who can deliver their presents but are still not in harmony with the flow of prosperity. They recognize their gifts and talents and even manage to put them in motion, but everything becomes more complicated when money is involved. It is as though there is a block that prevents them from giving what they have to give. In this case, there is an unconscious "no" to prosperity, which means there is probably an image, a belief in relation to money. There is difficulty to deal with this energy.

Pacts of vengeance

If you are already aware of your gifts and talents but somehow feel impeded from putting them into action, if you do not feel confident to do what you want to even though you know you can do it, be attentive for the possibility of being a prisoner of a vengeance pact. Deep down, always when there is a block in the flow of vital energy (depression, sadness, laziness, anger, fear), this means that there is a vengeance pact.

Pacts of vengeance are agreements the individual makes unconsciously when he or she is hit by shocks of exclusion, humiliation, rejection and repression. They are like contracts made between the ego and the lower Self. The lower Self matrices operate as guardians of these contracts, maintaining the empire of the false Self. They uphold the pacts of vengeance yet are also fed by them at the same time.

These unconscious agreements may express themselves in different ways in your life, such as lack of self-confidence, feeling of powerlessness, rebelliousness and victimism, among many other distortions. Even the lack of faith can be a symptom of a vengeance pact against the divine as you often blame God for your suffering. And when you blame yourself, vengeance shows itself as self-destruction, self-sabotage and self-hate.

Pacts of vengeance can be recognized through contradictions. For example, you dream of improving as a professional and want to prosper but fail to do what is needed for your dream to come about. The fact is that you think that you want that but deep down you don't, and that is exactly why you don't achieve it. There is an unconscious "no" that is blocking the flow of prosperity in your life.

If you are able to identify this contradiction, i.e. if you can see the signs of a vengeance pact appearing in the form of a lack of self-confidence, if you manage to see your insecurity when, in some way, you do not take advantage of the opportunities that appear in your life, you are reaching a very important point, a point of transformation. Identifying the activity of a "no" is like identifying an internal monster that may have been sucking your vital energy for a long time. However, this monster is still only a foot soldier in the battalion of the lower Self. For sure there is a general behind him, giving the orders. Therefore, by reaching this point, you need to immerse yourself in the self-investigation process to be able to identify this general and end this contract with evil.

PROSPERITY

True prosperity can only come when we are free from the pacts of vengeance related to it and from the fear of scarcity, which is another aspect of the lower nature that needs to be identified and understood.

Prosperity is born from trust. A prosperous person doesn't fear any kind of lack. He or she is always relaxed because they are not concerned about money. Obviously, it is needed to do the accounts and honor commitments, but it is not necessary to worry about it. Being prosperous does not necessarily mean having a bank account filled with a lot of money. Prosperity has nothing to do with the amount of money you have but rather with the trust that all your needs will be met regardless of this. Money arises as a natural consequence of this trust.

I have already spoken about wealth that is built through the fear of poverty. This is a wealth that creates stress because even if one has lots of money, this doesn't allow them to relax and enjoy their goods. This happens precisely because they don't trust that life will supply their needs. These people are always insecure and fear that something is going to lack. As a result, they are incapable of enjoying or sharing what they have.

On this point I want to stress a very important question that needs to be understood: prosperity survives from sharing. You cannot be truly prosperous unless you share what is received. You can accumulate money and knowledge, have lots of talents and ideas, but if you do not share them (which means not putting them into motion), the flow of prosperity will inevitably be blocked.

You need to learn to give just as you receive. This is because prosperity is a flow of energy, which means it is in constant movement. A flow is something that is passing, but when you try to grab it for yourself alone, this flow ends up being obstructed. If you don't share what you receive, the flow is obviously blocked.

People who are usually more afraid of not receiving are those who are least able to give. Fear makes them not trust that they will receive in return what they have to give. As a result, they give nothing and end up receiving nothing. This is one of the symptoms of fear of scarcity, which is a consequence of the lack of trust.

Trust is a virtue of the soul, a mature fruit of the tree of consciousness. It is born from a purified heart. You cannot forge this state with the mind. What you can do is dedicate yourself to self-knowledge so that you can access the images and beliefs* that prevent you from trusting.

Genesis of insecurity

In my studies as a psychologist and experience as a seeker and spiritual master, everything that I could research led me to the conclusion that fear of scarcity arises mainly from the relationship with the mother or with the feminine. The relationship with the father also bears an influence, but this happens later. The first influences occur through the mother since she is the portal through which we arrive here. This means we can state that primordial insecurity is born from a distortion of the feminine and is perpetuated mainly through the distortion of the masculine. Let us understand this better.

Regardless of the gender of our bodies, we all have a masculine and a feminine side to us. Life in this plane manifests itself in the balance between these two opposing principles, the masculine and the feminine. Just as it manifests itself in nature, such polarity exists in the human being.

We all have masculine and feminine virtues that, when distorted, are transformed into what we call "defects." For example, strength is a masculine quality that expresses itself as

---

* See **Key Practice 1:** Identifying dissatisfactions, contradictions and beliefs (p. 115).

aggressiveness and a desire for domination when distorted. Trust, for its part, is a feminine quality that appears as insecurity or submission when distorted. The distortion of the feminine feeds on the distortion of the masculine and vice-versa.

In my understanding, trust is the female quality that is most needed for the process of awakening love. Without it, self-realization is impossible. Trust is intimately related to love. If you do not trust, you do not love since trust is like a bridge to love. If you look at human relationships, you will see that love does not grow if there is no trust. If the relationship is contaminated by the lack of trust, even if only for a small part, it makes it impossible for love to grow.

I have been saying that romantic relationships are the best measuring tool for us to know where we are on the evolutionary journey. Through them, we can see how we are in relation to our parents who represent the female and male principles within us. In romantic relationships, trust or the lack of it is very clear, and the best way of measuring this is to see how much freedom we can give the other person, how much love is affected by the other's attitude.

The mother is certainly the biggest symbol within the feminine sphere. And our connection with the feminine through the mother is something really deep: she is the vehicle through which we have arrived on this terrestrial plane. There is now scientific proof that a child receives all the environmental impacts while still inside the mother's womb. This is not just from what occurs around her but also from what occurs in the mother's psycho-emotional world, including all her doubts, fears, joy and sadness. We stay within the mother's womb for nine months and, as a result, experience the world for the first time through her. We start receiving the first external influences through mother's milk. Sometimes the milk arrives with a taste of rejection, impatience and anger, and sometimes the milk doesn't arrive. Beliefs start being formed from then on and the fear of scarcity begins to be set up in our system.

This means that fear of scarcity is not related only to the lack of money but also to the lack of feeling embraced, lack of tenderness, of care—with the lack of love. This fear of not being loved manifests itself as a feeling of not belonging, insufficiency, powerlessness and inadequacy, amongst other negative feelings. And these feelings translate into beliefs that constantly say: "I can't get what I need" or "I don't deserve what I need." These beliefs function as orders to the subconscious and, as a result, we end up creating our reality. Based on these commands, situations in life that reinforce these beliefs begin to occur and set off a vicious circle.

The opposite is also true. When the milk is loving, i.e. when the child receives the information that it is being well fed, embraced, received and cared for, trust begins to be installed in its system. A core of faith is installed within you and makes it difficult for your self-confidence to be shaken.

As the contact with the mother is such a determining feature in the formation of this base of self-confidence, I always stress the need for reconciliation with the feminine, not only in the mother's form, but also in the form of nature, the human body and of women in general. We need to relearn to trust. I say relearn because we are born trusting, but our trust is broken at some point and we learn to feel fear.

Fear is like a super virus. There is no specific remedy for it, and it is very difficult to treat. We have been trying to cure ourselves from fear for a long time. And when we have the impression that we are free from it, situations often arise in life that make fear come back at full strength. At these moments, it is worth recalling that these situations serve precisely to expand our perception to the point where we can identify the fear traps before falling into them. This perception is only possible when we free ourselves from the belief that we cannot receive what we need. And this is only possible through forgiveness. As long as we haven't forgiven our mothers, we won't forgive the feminine and, if we don't forgive the feminine, we will continue to destroy the planet and our own lives.

When you reconcile yourself with the feminine through forgiveness, fear no longer has power over you. And if fear no longer has power, hate also becomes powerless because hate only has power through fear. Hate and fear walk hand-in-hand, but the base is fear. The shadow of the mother (distortion of the feminine) awakens fear in you and, through this fear, it awakens hate and the pain that comes with it. Hate perpetuates itself through the shadow of the father (distortion of the masculine). Therefore, if your consciousness is identified with the shadow of your parents, you inevitably feel the pain of neediness. Many other symptoms arise from neediness: jealousy, envy, competition, powerlessness, greed and all kinds of misery. But if your consciousness is identified with the light of your parents, you understand that this shadow is an illusion, and everything is transformed.

I feel that some questions are important to the ones who are in the path of self-knowledge and self-realization: When did I lose trust? When did I start to doubt and have fear? How can I trust? These are major questions that can help you map the beliefs that sustain fear.

Sometimes you take a step in the direction of trust and say: "Okay, I am going to trust!" Then you decide to follow the commands of your heart, but if something does not work out the way you had imagined, you become frustrated and stop trusting once again. Sometimes learning to trust means breaking a leg because you need to undergo an experience like this to free yourself from fear and let your self-confidence grow. The fact is that there is no guarantee that things are always going to be the way you expect them. Running risks is part of learning trust. Gradually, you will reach a place of internal self-confidence in which doubts end and you are sure you are in the right place, even when everything seems to be wrong. This is true trust, i.e. it does not depend on what is happening in the external world, since it comes from within. This trust removes any seed of doubt and ensures that all your needs will be met. It frees your system from fear, especially the fear of scarcity.

Money is energy

We have seen that fear of scarcity is related to a number of elements, not only money, and the deepest original fear is of not being loved. However, there is no doubt that one of the most important unfoldings of fear of scarcity is the fear of not having enough money and material resources.

Money is a powerful energy of exchange. In order to receive this energy, we need to offer something for it. We do something to receive it and use it according to our needs, which also creates a determined kind of energy. Nevertheless, money is a neutral energy: in itself it is neither positive nor negative. What determines its quality is the use and the value we give it. Just as money can help us undertake the journey, it can also make it very difficult and even destroy us. This is because we can easily transform it into greed, obsession for power and avarice that can develop into various other distortions. So what determines whether this energy will act in a negative or positive way in our lives is our ability to deal with it, which means handling the psycho-emotional content we project onto money.

If we look at the world economic situation, for example, we can see that humankind is having great difficulty in dealing with this energy. Greed has turned us into channels of cruelty beyond measure. Even with so much money in circulation and the abundance of natural resources, a large part of the population still suffers from misery and hunger. A small minority holds most of the planet's wealth while the majority still fights for survival. The misuse of this so powerful energy has become a threat to the evolutionary process of humankind.

There are many beliefs about money that end up transforming this energy into something more than it really is. We give money an extremely high emotional value. We project issues onto it that have nothing to do with its function in the world. This occurs because of distortions that create beliefs and images in relation to money. For example, when parents cannot give affection, tenderness and attention to their child, they try to fulfill this lack of love by buying them things. This makes the child relate affection to money. As a result, money ceases to have a practical use and becomes a symbolic need. It stops being a mere element of exchange and becomes something that makes up for affective neediness.

Another example is the belief, mentioned previously, that money buys everything, including happiness. Common sense tells us that having money is synonymous with being successful in life. There are other indicators of success but this belief leads us to feel that having lots of money is the basis for a successful life. We are programmed to believe from an early stage that we need success to be happy and, therefore, we need money. We need to "succeed in life," which means having professional recognition, fame and, above all, money.

Winning in Life

Therefore, money became a sign of success and a symbol of victory. I can only win if I have money, and if I don't have it I am a loser, a failure. This is common sense in terms of success, but this concept needs to be reviewed for obvious reasons. We need to redefine success. We have already enough proof that the search for the kind of success that depends on accumulating money has led us to failure. Our history, like the current state of the planet, shows that we have failed in our attempts to achieve happiness. The fact is that we have never been so unhappy. We have never been so depressed, poor, lost, confused, anxious, ill. This is not winning, this is failing.

The main cause of this failure is that we have forgotten our spiritual identity and we are unconscious about life's greater purpose. When we are disconnected from ourselves and our purpose, we act as if the body is the final reality and, in turn, we are guided by the body's impulses. We are unaware of the existence of a spiritual principle that permeates all existence and is superior to the material world, so we naturally surrender to the laws that govern this material world. This leads to the feeling that the meaning of life is to satisfy bodily needs. This is a complete distortion of reality. This idea that we are only a body without a soul unleashes successive waves of distortion, and it is from this that we create all the systems that regulate life within society.

Similarly, as we do not see the soul that inhabits us, we do not see the soul that inhabits the other person. We only see the body and judge everything by appearances. As we are incapable of seeing the soul behind every creation, we easily objectify life, transforming everything into consumer products. We can easily sell everything to obtain more money. If we can't see the soul of a tree, of a mountain, of a river, if we don't know the spiritual laws that rule life on this earthly plane, we only respect the material laws that are related basically to the need for survival.

And if the only reason for life is survival, human and spiritual values no longer make sense. According to this way of thinking, what matters is to have power over the other person and the material world. In the struggle for survival, the superior devours the inferior. And there is no species on this planet with the same feeling of superiority as the human being. Man regards himself as superior to everything and puts everything at the service of his survival. And when we believe that we are superior to other human beings, we turn them into slaves to satisfy our needs.

In this game of superiority and inferiority, it is the ego that rules. It is always comparing and judging based on the false idea of self. The human ego is completely sick, consumed by egoism. It only manages to see itself or what it considers belongs to it. All the ego does is to satisfy its personal needs or, at most, to satisfy the family (which is also at the service of its own needs). The ego is ruled by the fear of scarcity and does everything to accumulate money in the belief that, by doing so, it will ensure survival, protection and safety.

This despair in accumulating money and material goods arises from the forgetfulness about the true identity. As we are not aware of who we are, we run after material power without establishing any connection with the purpose of the soul. This distortion has led us to failure and suffering. We are always frustrated and constantly wanting something more. This happens because survival is not actually sufficient for the complex being that is the human being. Survival is sufficient for the body, but it is not sufficient for the soul that inhabits the body. The soul can only feel fulfilled when its program is realized.

We need to find a balancing point. The journey has to be self-sustainable. Matter and spirit must harmonize. It is true that our basic survival needs must be met, and we also need money to do so, but the fact is that money is only a tool, a means and not an end. These distortions have made it an end. Money has transformed itself into something much greater than it really is.

The question is to know why we are running after money. What and who does this money serve? If we only live to obtain money and meet our basic needs, we will inevitably experience anxiety about the lack of meaning in life. But when money is a consequence of the realization of the purpose of the soul, when it is at the service of self-realization, it transforms itself into a powerful tool that can make the journey much easier.

Recognizing "no's"

Two opposing forces act simultaneously within the individual up to a certain stage in evolution. One is the life impulse, which is conscious and moves in the direction of construction, union and love and which I usually call the affirmative current or, simply, "yes." The other is the death impulse, which is unconscious and moves in the direction of destruction, disunion and hate, which I usually call the negative current or, simply, "no."

These two opposing forces often act simultaneously in relation to a same situation or area of life. When the affirmative current is moving freely (meaning that there are no "no's" blocking the energy flow), we feel blessed and lucky. Everything happens naturally, without much effort, and we achieve a lot of things with the minimum of movement. In this case, we are in harmony with the law of least effort. And when the negative current is predominant, the exact opposite happens: things do not move and we feel blocked. We make great efforts to realize little and at times we do not move at all.

If the affirmative current is acting in your financial life, money is not a problem and everything you need comes easily. But if there is a "no" acting in this area, you do everything that is within your reach, but the money does not arrive or it is never enough and disappears when you least expect it. If the negative current is active in this area, no matter how much you try to control the mechanics of the flow of money in your life, you end up in the red at the end of the month without knowing how you reached this point.

When the "no" is acting in a stronger way in a certain area of life, negative situations repeat themselves and you cannot understand why. As the negative current is unconscious, it acts in a subliminal way. You don't see its activity, which occurs in the form of self-sabotage, so you betray yourself without noticing it. It is precisely because you don't notice its acting that you end up falling into another trap of the lower nature, which is an offshoot of the same "no:" victimhood. You start finding people to blame for your difficulties and become distracted in the game of accusations. The negative current acts as a self-deceit and creates an enchantment, a spell: you lose yourself in the mind games and the negative emotions that it creates because many thoughts and emotions need to be created to sustain this fantasy that you are a victim who has been treated unfairly.

What decides how these two opposite currents operate is *karma*. Some people are born with their financial lives resolved while others go through their lives having great difficulty in this area. If there is a "yes," i.e. if there are no marks from the past that appear as blockages to the flow of energy in the financial area, for instance, then there is prosperity and material abundance in your life. In this case, you trust and know that you will always have everything you need at the time you need it. But if there is a "no" in this area, you are tormented by the fear of scarcity. And this fear ends up really creating scarcity. You unconsciously attract scarcity and, as a result, confirm the belief that you are unable to get what you need. When this happens, you are taken by anger and skepticism and believe that you have reasons to complain and get revenge. As a result, the "no" gradually becomes even stronger and a vicious circle is established.

The "no" is like a *karmic* knot, an energetic blockage created by shocks of pain that, for their part, have created beliefs and frozen images in the system. Such blockages that prevent the natural flow of vital energy create distortions and can only be dissolved through self-investigation as it is only when we manage to identify the beliefs that sustain the "no's" that we can free ourselves from them.

In the courses of The Path of the Heart, the psycho-spiritual method of self-knowledge I have developed, different ways of identifying these beliefs and frozen images are proposed. And starting from this identification, the process of reconverting the flow of vital energy begins. At some point in the past this natural flow of vital energy was distorted and transformed into the death impulse. It is only through self-knowledge that the "no" can be transformed into "yes." And the first step to this is the recognition of the existence of the "no." Before anything else, you need to recognize that there is a part of you that is playing against yourself, i.e. a part of you that doesn't want things to get better. There is an internal voice that is constantly saying "no" to prosperity, to joy, to union and to love.

I know that it is often difficult to believe that one is choosing unhappiness, but I repeat that if you find it difficult to achieve or obtain something you desire a lot, this means there is a contradiction within you: on one hand you want it, but on another, you don't. One of the ways of recognizing this internal contradiction is by observing the size of the effort you need to make to realize what you consciously desire. There is a psychic law that states that the more frantically you run after something and it still manages to escape from your hands or seems to flee from you, the greater is your unconscious "no" for what you consciously desire so much. And the greater the effort, the greater is your inability to deal with this "no."

The difficulty of dealing with the "no" is due exactly to the fact that it is unconscious. You cannot deal with it because it is outside your field of perception. It appears that you want to be a self-confident person but without noticing (unconsciously), you create situations in which you feel insecure. So you return to the same pattern of insecurity and you continue to be jealous and envious. This happens because the fact that the belief is unconscious expands the power it has over your psyche. An unconscious impulse is like a criminal who attacks you from behind in the dark. It is like an invisible adversary against whom you have no defenses because you cannot see it. That is why, even when the "no" represents only a small portion of energy, it always ends up knocking you down because you are taken by surprise.

The "no" is a saboteur of happiness, and the process of identifying this self-saboteur is not so simple. Humility and courage are needed, as well as a lot of determination, in order to see it. You need to be really committed to truth as pride, in the form of vanity, will be hurt at some point. For vanity, it is difficult to admit that you are in hell as a result of your own choice. It is difficult to admit that you are where you put yourself. However, when you finally manage to recognize and admit that you are the one who chooses not to realize your dreams and desires, you can start the process of transforming your contradictions—and the "no" begins to transform itself into "yes."

I have inspired all those who are with me to look for the roots, the foundations of the "no" within themselves.* I have

---

* See **Key Practice 1:** Identifying dissatisfactions, contradictions and beliefs (p. 115).

suggested they try to identify the beliefs that sustain self-deceit and self-sabotage. For this reason, I suggest that they try to remember the lies and stories they told themselves and that even today uphold these beliefs. Ask yourself why you created a certain situation. Why is it that you don't manage to achieve what you want so much? Why do you have this "no?"

Make the cause and effect relation between the past and present moment, trying to identify the situations that marked you and have an influence in your life even today. Perhaps you will be surprised when you identify a belief that insists in making you believe that, in your case, it is not possible to have prosperity, joy and love. By doing so, you will begin to decipher the symbols that are present in these stories from the past and which relate to the *karma* seen at the present moment.

If you can undertake this process of self-investigation, understanding that everything that is seen in the present moment is the result of a choice of yours, a new outlook on life will open up for you. This is because the difficulties will start to be seen as opportunities for growth—chances to free yourself from the *karmic* knots and settle accounts with the past. In other words, these are opportunities for ascension.

Suffering to be happy

One of the manifestations of the internal saboteur of happiness and prosperity is the belief that you need to suffer to be happy. This belief unfolds in a number of ways: it begins with the idea that you need to work a lot and make great efforts to get a day off; that you need to make lots of sacrifices so that one day you will be able to relax (because enjoying life is something for vagrants); and that in order to be a spiritual person you need to make vows of poverty . . . No matter how unaware we may be of such beliefs, they are buried deep in our system. They have been operating for so long that we are unable to see how much they still influence our choices and how they keep us addicted to suffering.

The life model in which people need to work a lot, receive little and relax even less is obviously a result of the forgetfulness of the purpose of life. As I mentioned previously, money has stopped being a means through which we can enjoy life and has become an end in itself, since being successful is synonymous with having money. This means that we started spending most of our time pursuing money, but we don't have time to enjoy what it provides to us. Even though many people work hard, they do not even receive enough to enjoy and have a comfortable life. Most are only ensuring their survival.

Some people become rich with the aim of being able to stop working so hard one day so they can then relax and take it easy in some quiet spot. They wait for old age to arrive in order to start living life. Some of them reach old age and continue to work hard even though they don't have any material need because they are afraid of dealing with the lack of having something to do. Another belief that is also an offshoot of the belief that we need to suffer to be happy is that we are what we do. This means we cannot relax because we have always to be doing something.

You must already have heard popular sayings like: "The early bird catches the worm" or "It's easier for a camel to pass through the eye of a needle than for a rich man to enter the kingdom of God." These are expressions of mental conditioning that are deeply rooted in the human psyche. They are beliefs that have been installed in our system through guilty and religious morality. It is as though we needed to be crucified and have a crown of thorns placed on our head to be able to enter the kingdom of heaven. In other words, we need to make great sacrifices to deserve happiness.

I see a great denial of money, especially among spiritual seekers. This is a kind of moralism in relation to prosperity and results in them being put in tremendously difficult situations. Many of them even become used to the lack of things and convince themselves that spiritual life needs to be austere, but they end up depending on other people to supply their needs. Some switch off from practical questions of life (they stop working and move to a spiritual community) in the belief that they need to do this in order to find the true purpose, but they end up suffering with scarcity. This is not intelligent. It is a trick of the shadow to perpetuate suffering.

While you are still unsure of your purpose, you may perhaps need to continue working to meet your needs. If you really are not in the right place and you came into the world to do something very different from what you are doing today, you will have to make a move at some point, but this transition needs to occur naturally. This change may need to happen quickly, and you may need to leave everything, but there are no doubts in this case as it is your heart that is telling you to act like that. You are not running away or fooling yourself. You are confident that you are on the right path. Nevertheless, it is best not to act precipitately if it is still not clear because by doing so you are only creating more *karma*. Furthermore, someone will still have to pay your bills.

Material prosperity and self-realization are not opposed to each other. Money does not hold back spiritual evolution. If we want to create a culture of peace and prosperity, we need to rid our minds of these limiting beliefs. Violence and fear of scarcity are intimately related. Peace is impossible if most of the population is suffering with any lack. Spiritual values cannot be developed if most people still do not have their basic needs met.

For all this, we need to harmonize ourselves with this energy that is money. We should not overvalue or undervalue it. Some people regard money as God, whereas others think it is the devil. Some devote their whole lives to accumulating money, while others cannot even have money in their wallets as they do not want to be contaminated by it. We need to find a balancing point.

When you get down to it, money has become a great taboo like sex. Many people are guilty about money because it can lead to certain pleasures in life. The fact is that pleasure is the human beings' greatest taboo.

It is certain that we are not incarnated here just to pursue pleasure since pleasure in this plane is actually a state that occurs in the interval between two pains. I know that this might seem pessimistic, but it is just realistic. Pain is part of this material experience on Earth, but, just as pain is intrinsic to you, pleasure is also a natural right of every being incarnated in a body. At some time, you need to harmonize yourself with pleasure because it is also part of the realization of the higher purpose of life: self-realization. At some point we will experience life's greatest pleasure, which is bliss or lasting happiness.

A pearl of wisdom accredited to Buddha is that pain is inevitable but suffering is unnecessary. Not being necessary means it is optional. By being incarnated in a body, we inevitably experience some pain, but the continuance of this pain is a question of choice. Pain has a function on the evolutionary plane. It serves to teach us some lessons and to awaken us from numbness and the dream of attachment, fear, lust and lack of love. However, the suffering generated by hurts, resentment, vengeance, drama, complaints and accusations is unnecessary.

We should recall that we will live in this body for a very short period. Time is the most valuable thing we have. Life passes when you least expect it and the game is over. That is why you should not waste your time with useless things. Don't fall for the illusion that you need to fight a lot so you can enjoy life one day. You don't need to conquer the world to be happy. You can be happy now, even without having conquered the world.

Prosperity and service

Another offshoot of the "no" for prosperity is the idea that the purpose of the soul can only be realized through social work or charity, something that does not involve receiving money. This happens because people confuse the fulfillment of purpose with voluntary service. This is known in the yoga tradition as *seva*, selfless service that is a practice of *Karma Yoga*, the yoga of action.

First of all, it should be understood that by aligning our actions with the internal purpose, regardless of what we are doing or receiving in exchange for our work, we will always be at the service of a higher purpose. As we have seen, the soul's purpose is always related to the higher purpose as it is at its service. Therefore, your soul's program may involve voluntary work in a charitable institution or spiritual community, but you will not feel you are missing anything in this case. You will feel complete and happy on waking every day to carry out your work. However, if you carry out a voluntary service and feel your needs are not being met or you are suffering from the fear of scarcity, this may not be your path.

You can serve and be aligned with the higher purpose while working for a large company and receiving a good salary. What really matters is the internal fit, i.e. whether your action in the world makes sense. You can do *seva* anywhere, even in the big city centers. I have said before that spirituality today needs to be practical, which means it must be sustainable. *Seva*, or selfless service, is a way of spiritually practicing the purification of the ego, which, even though it involves action, is an internal practice. If your actions are full of the consciousness of purpose, they will be transformed into a spiritual practice serving the higher good.

Not every voluntary service will be aligned with the purpose of the soul, particularly if you use it as a way of escaping from the world or from what you really need to do. It is true that by putting your gifts and talents at the service of a common good through a voluntary service or a donation, you are working for *dharma*, the higher ´ purpose. Nevertheless, it is not always part of your soul's program to carry out a work of this nature, precisely because you need to earn money to align with your purpose.

You can carry out *seva* and be materially prosperous at the same time. When you find harmony with your purpose, your material needs are naturally met. If *seva* is aligned with your mission, with what you have come to do in the world, you will inevitably have everything you need. This is a law.

You can also be aligned to the purpose and still experience some kind of lacking, but this occurs because some adjustments still need to be made. The ego may have hijacked your action, so you still need to work to purify some aspect that you don't understand. The fact is that if your action in the world is aligned with the purpose of your soul and, in turn, with the higher purpose, it is a divine manifestation. It means that Existence is carrying out the game through you and by being in harmony with Existence it is impossible to go through lack. Lack arises when an aspect of the ego enters the game and steals the scene.

By carrying out your individual purpose, you are at the service of the collective purpose and you are always where you are supposed to be when this happens. If the Mystery puts you in an *ashram* for some reason, you meditate and pray with joy. If it takes you to a social institution, working to cure the world, you do what has to be done with satisfaction. If you need to be in a large city, working for the government, running a big company or dedicating yourself to the education of your children, you do what needs to be done with enthusiasm. Wherever you are, you know that you need to be where you are. What you are doing stops being a compulsion of the ego and becomes a service for the greater good.

CONSCIOUSNESS OF PURPOSE

Being conscious or aware of purpose is synonymous with being aware of service, because your purpose is nothing more than the service you have come to provide to humanity. And understanding this is the greatest blessing a human being can receive in life. However, this awareness is a flowering, and, like a flower that blooms naturally, this phenomenon only occurs when your personality is duly prepared. This means you have already purified fear and hate in your system to a certain point.

Many people become anxious about this issue, and this concern transforms itself into an obstacle for the revelation of the purpose. However, you need to understand that the awareness of the program of your soul is a process that works in its own time. You may still not be aware of what you have come here to do but are living the experiences needed so this purpose will be revealed to you at some point. You may be doing a lot of things for egoistic reasons, but they serve as a preparation for this. The greater Self that inhabits you often takes you to certain places, to undergo certain experiences and learn certain lessons that will serve for your maturity— and maturity is an essential quality for the expansion of consciousness. We could say that this preparation, this maturing process, is one of the stages of the realization of your soul's program even though you may not be aware of it.

The program of the soul is unique. Every soul arrives on this plane with a vision, something very specific to be shared with the world. And even though, until a certain moment, this program is split into different phases, it remains unique.

The soul is wise—it knows, understands and respects the laws of life. It knows you need to be whole in any initiative if you are to be successful in it. All your energy needs to be focused in one direction because if you are heading in different ways you will end up hurting yourself. Therefore, your program often needs to be carried out in stages, and these stages develop according to the expansion of consciousness.

The development of your skills or latent potentials is also part of this same preparation process, so you can give what you have to offer. Nonetheless, some of these skills can only be recognized and developed when we are aware of what we came here to fulfill. Often when you become aware of your program, you start to see sense in skills you had already discovered but had still not dedicated yourself to developing them. When you become aware of the purpose, your talents usually modify and multiply as they are the mechanism, the tool through which purpose is fulfilled.

If there is anything that can bring this feeling of completeness to the human being, it is the awareness of the soul's purpose. And purpose begins to reveal itself as you surrender to the spiritual flow that is synonymous with surrendering yourself to the commands of the heart. The realization of purpose is the manifestation of divinity through you. As you mature and gradually de-identify from the false Self, you become an instrument, a channel of divinity. You gradually become a silent witness who only observes divinity working through you. And divinity uses your gifts and talents to realize the greater purpose.

Action and donation

By developing our gifts and talents, which are the abilities we were born with, even if they are still being used to carry out the whims of the ego, our actions start being delivered with unparalleled efficiency. The result of the actions that are born from our natural gifts is always filled with extra beauty and shine. And when the awareness of the greater purpose of these actions exists, the result is particularly enlightening because they gain an even more special quality. Being aware of the purpose is knowing your place in the world and your part in the divine plan. You know you are where you should be. It is like a part of a jigsaw puzzle that becomes something bigger when it fits into place. And this fit allows your actions to gain this new quality—the quality of service or donation.

The soul's purpose is intimately related to service. We could say that service and purpose are the same, as serving means being a tool that undertakes the greater purpose of expanding consciousness. Serving is becoming a channel of love to make the other grow, prosper, be happy; in order to make the other shine. When you activate your purpose, i.e. putting it into motion, you become an inspiration for others, a channel for the expansion of the collective consciousness. Service means putting love into action, i.e. letting love pass through you to reach another.

Seva is a donation, even if this donation has been carried out through a profession in which there is a financial agreement. In this case, money is the result of the activation of your purpose and is not in first place—awareness of service is in first place.

A wise saying that was born from the Christian tradition states that "It is by giving that you receive." This is true, but it only happens if the donation is made in a selfless way. This benign circle of giving and receiving is completed only when you give without wanting anything in return. This is the only way energy can circulate. And service is only selfless when one renounces the result of one's actions, i.e. when you can do something without expecting recognition, attention, fame or money. This is the only way possible to experience the power of service.

We are talking about a spiritual law (not a moral law created by human mind): the more you give, the more you receive. When this happens, your energy is increasingly more activated through the energy of the other and vice-versa. And when your energy grows, you experience joy, fullness and connection with the higher reality. You feel increasingly more guided since the more you hear and follow the commands of your heart, the more it speaks to you.

Having developed the quality of service, you begin to walk the path of surrender. Your learning at this stage is to deliver the fruits of your actions to the great Mystery, which means going beyond the ego, beyond authorship. You stop doing things to promote your personality or to feed your vanity.

But when this quality has still not been developed and doing things is still automatic and driven by egoistic interests, speaking about the renunciation of the fruits of the actions can even appear to be offensive. This happens because the ego still needs to receive recognition for what it does. It still needs to add value to the false identity. However, there is nothing wrong with this. It is a natural step and is necessary within the process of the evolution of the soul, as you need to have something to renounce. If you don't have anything to renounce, what then will you be renouncing? You need to have an ego to surrender. The surrender of a king has a different value from that of a beggar.

It is very important not to fool yourself: there is nothing wrong in wanting recognition for what you do. It all depends on what your soul needs at that moment. There is also nothing wrong in wanting to be important or earning money. Many people are led to serve in important positions, in politics or in the financial market—at the center of the *matrix*. Who are we to judge the designs of Existence? Each one is where they need to be. And being where one needs to be means we are in place even when there is no consciousness of the greater purpose in this yet.

If I was to choose the most powerful tool for ascension, I would say it is service. When you allow yourself to serve without wanting anything in return, you feel immediate satisfaction. I know it may sound contradictory because I am saying the value of the service is in not wanting anything in return and claiming, at the same time, that your heart is immediately filled with satisfaction and joy by serving. Some people will obviously try to serve to experience this joy. However, by doing so they will face the need to purify another center of egoism within them because they are still doing it with some interest, even if it is to feel joy.

Nevertheless, there is nothing wrong in beginning this way. You start from your interest in experiencing joy and, based on this, you can identify the points that need to be purified. You will gradually be purifying these points until you can really surrender to service in a selfless way. You will reach the point when you can do it only for love. And it is this service undertaken for love that brings fullness and happiness without cause.

Action and prayer

Spiritual awareness needs to expand in everyone and everywhere because this is the greatest goal of life. For that to happen, spirituality needs to be part of everyone's life. The spiritual message needs to arrive everywhere—in companies, public institutions and schools. This is one of the positive aspects of the interactive age: the great possibility of sharing the spiritual message. Long ago, people had to leave work, their family and the comfort of the home to live in a monastery or in a cave in the Himalayas to have access to spiritual knowledge. We now live in a time in which knowledge is increasingly more accessible to everyone. There is obviously a negative aspect to this as the message loses its sparkle and a superficial form of spirituality may also be created. However, I am optimistic about this as we can deal with this superficiality as a phase or a seed that has been planted. If true spirituality will flower, we cannot control it.

As I have said before, the time has come when spirituality needs to be practical. It is no longer necessary (or even possible) to be in an *ashram* to pray, meditate and connect with the Mystery. The opposite in fact: it has become necessary to learn to do this wherever we are. To do so, we need to make a prayer to the universe out of every combination of actions. I see *seva* as a practical form of prayer, an expression of surrender to the Divine, a practical form of declaring your love to the Mystery.

This is the essence of *Karma Yoga,* the path to freedom through selfless action. Yoga means union—union with the greater reality that lives within us and permeates our whole life. Therefore, *Karma Yoga* is uniting oneself with the All through action. And we can be increasingly more united with the All when we renounce the ego. When we are able to give up the need to grow as individuals, we enter the collective sphere of growth, i.e. we begin transforming egoism into altruism, which is the highest form of love.

When every minute of action is transformed into prayer, your life becomes a constant practice of yoga. However, you need to develop totally in the action to do this, which means you must be totally focused and fully present, occupying your body in every attitude. This quality can be developed through meditation but also through *seva* itself.

While you are doing your *seva,* you are naturally directing the vectors of your will and disciplining your mind at the same time as you are purifying your system from egoism. The practice of *seva* also prepares you to access a higher sphere of love: altruism.

Nevertheless, it is natural that at some stage you will swing between altruism and egoism, precisely because the purification is not yet complete. You should also not deny egoism. It is important to recognize that it exists, but it is also important not to fuel it. You recognize that it is present but do not judge it. Observe the shadow but strengthen the light. By doing so, you give force to altruism, to the Higher Self.

You can then gradually see an internal alignment that shows itself in the form of a feeling of fulfillment, belonging, fitting in. You stop feeling isolated and divided and feel part of something greater. You transport yourself from the mind to the heart. Love passes through you and is scattered onto the world through your gifts and talents. By doing so, you become a link in the universal chain of life, in which everyone's stories are connected and in which destinies flow in the same direction. You become a servant of the Mystery.

This is my work. I am a servant of the Mystery. I am constantly praying for love to awake in everyone and everywhere.* I pray for everyone to be able to experience the main fragrance of true service, which is joy without cause. My praying is carried out in different ways, including through actions, attitudes and decisions, but mainly through the hands of those who are touched by this message and choose to commit themselves to the mission of awakening love. I am very grateful to those who have been offering their gifts and talents to serve this great goal. Gratitude, like joy without cause, is a flower that springs from the virtue of selfless service. May you be able to have this experience!

Service and cure

One of the features of the mission of the human soul is also to synthesize and transform the planetary shadow, which is the combination of the shadow of the individuals who live here. The matrices of the lower Self manifest themselves in every person, to a greater or lesser extent, and this manifestation also takes place on a collective level. Depending on where you are, you often notice there is a greater activity by a determined matrix in you. This happens because the collective unconscious influences the individual unconscious and vice-versa. That is why when you transform the shadow within you, the collective shadow is also transformed.

---

* See **Key Practice 7**: Praying to become a pure channel of love (p. 131).

However, for you to transform these dark aspects within and outside yourself, you need to take total responsibility for them, i.e. you need to consider them as being solely yours. It is true that evil is found everywhere, but you need to take responsibility for the evil that acts through you.

Self-responsibility is one of the elements of the cure process. When you take responsibility for the evil that acts through you and allow yourself to understand the mechanisms through which it manifests itself through your actions, the understanding of it will gradually grow until evil loses force and you no longer act on it.

Understanding is light and light immediately dissolves the shadow. It is part of the soul's noble mission to illuminate, understand and transform the dark aspects of humanity through the purification and transformation of the personality. This is the reason why the main focus of my work has been on the process of personal transformation because by lighting up the dark side that lives in you, you also illuminate the collective darkness. The planet becomes brighter with every point of light that is lit up within you. When you transform the pride inside you into humility, the world becomes humbler. When you transform the fear that exists inside you into trust, the world becomes more confident. The same happens to all the matrices of the lower Self. What I am saying here is that the planetary cure depends on the cure of every one of us.

As I mentioned previously, *seva* is a practice of purifying the ego. The purification process often becomes very difficult. It is like a washing machine that goes into spinning mode and the washing of *karmas* becomes extremely intense.

That is the time when the temptation to stop everything and run off is great. This occurs because this purification involves revisiting traumatic situations, reviving negative feelings and deep pains. This *karmic* washing involves a certain suffering because all the pain that was numb and hidden for a long time arises at this moment. And you experience again not only your pain, which is the product of your personal history, but also the pain that is the product of a collective *karma*. Collective suffering passes through your body to be transmuted and your own suffering is also transmuted as you surrender to this process.

Therefore, when the *karma yogi*, a healer, puts him or herself in service, they transform suffering into joy. I usually say that every *karma yogi* takes poison because his or her work is precisely to transform poison into nectar. When I say poison, I am referring to the evil that manifests itself as cruelty. It is through it that the forces that are against love operate in our system, both individually and collectively. Cruelty is made from fear and hate, and the pain is contained within it.

So you become a healer when you are ready to give up your own cruelty, your own illnesses. This means that you need to be willing to cure yourself. Because if you have not yet purified at least some of your own pains, you end up identifying with the pain of the other person and fail to free it. When this happens, the pain installs itself in your system and you become ill. However, if you are mature enough not to identify yourself with the pain that is passing through your system, you become a true curing instrument—you breathe in suffering and breathe out joy.

This is not something that you can learn in books but through practice. You learn to work for the other person as you make yourself available to serve. You can be cleaning or sweeping the floor for another person, but this is only the external aspect, the material aspect of your action. Deep down, you are sweeping *karmas*.

Any selfless action, made with the awareness of purpose, has this power of cure. There is no more powerful and valuable practice than serving. Therefore, serve everyone and love everyone. Work so that everyone can be happy, so everyone can be blissful, so everyone can be at peace. Wanting all this just for yourself is a great restraint on your life.

6. Transcendence

AWAKENING LOVE

At the end of the day, there is only one purpose. The individual soul's purpose is also that of all humanity and everything that exists, since it is related to the very essence of creation. Manifesting purpose means exhaling the fragrance of the Being that lives within us. And this fragrance is the love found sleeping inside us. The purpose can only show itself when we have awakened at least a part of this love. Purpose can only manifest itself when we have awoken at least some amount of this love. At the same time as love awakens, purpose gradually reveals itself, and as purpose reveals itself, love expands.

When I speak of love, I am referring to the true meaning of the word and not to the kind of love conditioned by the desires and whims of the ego. I am referring to real love, which is selfless and unconditional. Real love loves, regardless of what it receives in return. It does not depend on the love of the other to exist. It does not want rewards, promises and guarantees. It simply loves.

Serving and loving

When it comes down to basics, love is serving. There is a strong connection between love and service, as anyone who loves naturally serves and anyone who serves naturally loves. Just as there cannot be love without freedom, so there cannot be service without love. Loving and serving in a selfless way represent the highest form of consciousness that can exist on this planet.

Some people might feel this is even a little romantic, but it is the opposite. I am referring to the reality of our lives: we are not here to stroll about freely. We did not come here to go shopping in a mall, date a little, marry, leave some children in the world and then go away. We came to serve. And as long as we do not wake up to this reality, we will continue to fail in our attempts to find peace and happiness. As long as we think we are here only to satisfy the ego's desires, suffering will be our fate.

We came to serve, but I often only say that we came to love since it is easier to assimilate and understand. What happens is that many people regard service as a word with negative connotations. Serving is usually associated with doing something in a subordinate way, with a sense of inferiority. The ego becomes really upset with this. Furthermore, one of the elements to be purified through the practice of *seva* is precisely this pride, this lack of humility. It is the ego that feels inferior. It always wants to be in special positions, doing only nice things it regards as being more important. This is precisely what needs to be transformed.

The deeper meaning of this so badly-interpreted practice that is, in fact, one of the highest virtues of the soul must be understood. Serving selflessly represents a high level of spiritual development. However, particularly in the West where culture glorifies the ego and stokes an arrogant approach to things, serving is synonymous with downgrading. In India and other cultures where the main spiritual traditions are based on a master-disciple relationship, serving is among the most advanced and elevated practices.

I know that when I talk about selfless service, renouncing authorship and the result of the actions, spiritual surrender and a master-disciple relationship, I am touching on delicate matters, precisely because they are difficult to understand. The rational mind finds all this very mysterious. Some people will even have a certain aversion to these issues. This is because the mind and reason dominate the heart and intuition in places where the culture has been basically influenced by rationalism. The mind rationalizes and tries to understand, but it cannot because the mind cannot understand what lies beyond it, and certain aspects of spiritual surrender go well beyond the mind. The idea of a disciple surrendering to a master is something those whose mental structure has been firmly formed by reason and who are conditioned to the habit of putting questioning and doubt before knowing and trusting find extremely difficult to understand. Nevertheless, regardless of what the mind manages to understand, it is a fact that some souls come with the more specific purpose of serving a master.

Some people will serve through their profession, their personal or social projects, their art. Others will serve through surrendering themselves to a master, which means they will place their gifts and talents directly at the service of the mission they have come to undertake. Some among them will be led to be inside a spiritual community, living a life of renunciation, but there will be few of them because we are being called to integrate spirituality with the material life. Most spiritual seekers, even those under the guidance of a master, need to live their spirituality in a practical way that will allow them to be in the city, working in companies and looking after their family.

However, in contrast to what many people think, this way of life poses no obstacle to a deep relationship between a master and a disciple. The connection is often stronger when the person is not physically close to the master because this physical proximity not only creates stronger purifications but can also cause a series of projections that will become obstacles on the journey. This happens because some people do not understand the human dimension of the master and end up losing themselves in idealizations.

What matters is knowing that the master–disciple relationship does not depend on the physical presence precisely because it is a relationship that occurs on the spiritual plane. The meeting between a master and a disciple is an extremely rare and precious phenomenon that many people will not be able to have the privilege of experiencing precisely because it involves elements that go well beyond the limits of human reason. One of these elements is devotion.

Devotion is a sphere of unconditional love that is very little understood and judged by the skeptical mind. It is a more refined aspect of love that cannot be explained. It can only be experienced.

Only art can try and express what devotion represents, as it is a mystery to be unveiled by the heart. You cannot think about devotion, only feel it. You cannot convince anyone about devotion as it is something to be experienced.

When love matures, devotion flowers naturally. Your devotion can be focused on some divine form, image, name or master. However, the highest aspect of devotion is when love goes beyond form or personal issues and no longer has a specific focus. It is when you become a lover of divinity, a lover of life. And when this happens, service stops being a purification, a medicine you use to cure illnesses. Service flows simply because it has become the main reason for living.

However, many people confuse devotion with fanaticism, and this is a big mistake. Devotion and fanaticism are radically opposed dimensions. Devotion arises from the experience of truth and fanaticism from imagination. It is a product of the conditioned mind as it is based on beliefs: the person who does not know the truth believes in the truth, but it is the truth created by his or her own mind.

The fanatic believes he or she is the owner of the truth without even having had a glimpse of it. Deep down, this person is hiding from the Truth through a supposed faith. Any expression that denies his or her truth is seen as a threat. Anyone who does not believe what he or she believes in is seen as an enemy. And this occurs precisely because at bottom he is denying the Truth. His faith is based on borrowed beliefs and truths. It is a false faith.

Fanaticism is, therefore, an expression of the false Self. It hides itself behind a mask of the devotee and is nothing but a distortion of love.

The genuine devotee is the one who, having passed through the desert of skepticism and the proofs of doubt and questions that doubt brings, has a glimpse of the Truth. And it is through this experience that the devotee has developed the virtues of the true faith and selfless service that involves humility, acceptance and gratitude, as well as dedication, rectitude and focus. Whoever becomes a devotee of life wakes up in the morning and asks the Mystery: "How can I serve?" One places oneself at the disposition of the divinity in order to serve divinity in the form of all living beings, in the form of life. This is the deepest meaning of becoming a pure channel of love.* And this is what we can call spiritual surrender.

Common purpose

When devotion and selfless service meet, a powerful alchemy is formed. I have witnessed many beautiful manifestations arising from this combination, mainly when it occurs in a group of people. When one soul surrenders to fulfill the greater goal through love, this is really something of great value, but extraordinary things happen when many souls come together for the same purpose, driven by devotion.

Overcoming limitations and winning challenges is something extraordinary. It is to manifest light in the middle of darkness. It means to be able to love the other, even when that individual is being a channel of the deepest hate and ignorance. It is being united to the other even when everything leads to separation. This is transcendence, i.e. going beyond egoism and manifesting altruism. What enables the manifestation of what I am calling something extraordinary is union. There is no transcendence without union. Union can bring about genuine miracles because when we unite our forces (our potential and virtues) around the same goal, we become really powerful. This is the force that a *sangha* has, which is a community of people united around a spiritual master for the realization of a common purpose.

---

* See **Key Practice 7**: Praying to become a pure channel of love (p. 131).

The *sangha* is a living organism that expands as each individual member of the community gradually becomes cured and matures. As the *sangha* expands and strengthens, it transforms itself into a refuge of cure and connection for all those who are looking for the truth. That is why the *sangha* is regarded by Buddhists as one of the sacred jewels of the path of enlightenment.

The *sangha* is the body of the master. What allows the health of the master's body is the *sangha*'s capability to work in union, friendship and harmony since it is through the *sangha* that the master fulfills his or her mission in the world. A master can only realize his or her purpose through the realization of the purpose of those who accompany him or her, as part of the master's mission is to guide them to this realization. One of the aspects of a master's work is precisely to awaken the memory of purpose and activate the latent potentials of those who choose to follow the path with him or her, so that they may put themselves at service of the greater good. As this work is made and the disciples begin to donate their gifts and deliver the presents they have brought to the world, the master also receives presents, since the greatest present a spiritual master can have is to see the realization of his or her student.

Although the master plays the guiding role in the master-disciple relationship, both are growing together as one expands through the expansion of the other. When this movement occurs through the union of many souls, real quantum leaps of the expansion of collective consciousness become possible. Consciousness is synonymous with light, with enlightenment. The *sangha* operates like a great luminous bubble that, as it grows, dispels darkness. It is one of the most powerful instruments of the path of self-realization.

BEING LOVE

Self-realization or realization of oneself means becoming aware of who we are, awakening from the dream of separation created by the ego and returning to the perception of Unity. At the end of the day, realizing oneself means returning to your own loving essence: just as a river merges with the sea, so human consciousness merges with the divine consciousness. Consciousness is unique, but the illusory nature of this plane makes it seem fragmented.

As we have already seen, when we incarnate on Earth to live this material experience, through a body and an ego, we are wrapped in an illusory veil that makes us believe we are separated. Having an ego necessarily implies the existence of an idea of Self. Therefore, it is part of the game on this planet to have this sense of separation. It is part of the learning of the soul that is incarnated in the body to believe that it is a small drop of water whereas it is the ocean itself. And, as we believe we are a drop, we also forget about the ocean. In Hindu philosophy, the person who frees himself or herself from the illusion of separation and becomes aware of his or her true identity is called *jivanmukta* (free soul).

This is the path we are taking. The path of self-realization or freedom—the path where the drop meets the ocean. What makes this remembrance possible is the love that is awake. Without love there can be no expansion of consciousness. And without the expansion of consciousness, there can be no remembrance. Remembering means enlightening, bringing light to the field of vision. Forgetting means darkening, removing light from the field of vision. When we forget something, it is as though it didn't exist.

Love is the light that inhabits us. It is what moves us in this plane. All the evils of this world exist because love is asleep within us. When I say asleep, I am referring to an inactive state. It means that love is present but is asleep or inactive. Just as a seed that is not planted cannot transform itself into a tree and bear fruit, love that is asleep cannot fulfill its goal of expanding consciousness.

As a result, we have arrived at the end of our study with the conclusion that we are here to awaken the sleeping love. Not only in ourselves, but in all beings, also because love awakes in us when we want to see the other person awaken. I believe that at this point of the study it must be clear that it is only possible to shine when we work for the other to shine as well. We can only cure ourselves when we work for everyone to cure themselves. We can only realize our own purpose when we work for the realization of the purpose of the other.

Love is the seed and at the same time the mature fruit of the tree of consciousness. It is the very sap of life, it is our essence. Just as the rose's perfume is inseparable from the rose, so love is inseparable from the Being. When we truly love, we are exhaling the fragrance of the Being. Just as the purpose of the sun is to illuminate and provide warmth, the purpose of the human being is to love. That is why I always say that everything is summed up as love.

7. Key Practices

KEY PRACTICES

To help you gain an in-depth knowledge of the concepts treated in this book, I would like to suggest some practices that will allow you to really integrate the knowledge into your system in such a way that the content in this book does not only become accumulated information but rather wisdom. When knowledge transforms itself into wisdom, it stops being mental knowing and becomes the soul's knowing, which means that it becomes a virtue.

There is no point in knowledge if it is not put into practice. Life obviously provides the best opportunities for us to use this knowledge in practical terms, but certain practices can operate as real keys that open doors to new understanding and insights about your evolutionary process. Practice allows you to be more prepared to pass through the challenges of life, and it also speeds up the process of purifying the personality. As a consequence, consciousness expands.

Key Practice 1

Identifying dissatisfactions, contradictions and beliefs

As we have seen, the identification or the recognition of our dissatisfactions—and, in turn, our internal contradictions—is the first step towards the transformation of what we do not want or do not like in our lives. After all, it is only by identifying an illness that it can be healed. This acknowledgement seems pretty simple, but we are not always clear in relation to our dissatisfactions and far less so in respect to our contradictions, as we have ended up becoming used to certain negative situations.

The aim of this exercise is precisely to help us have greater clarity on what we would like to be different in our lives but, for some reason, we are unable to change. This clarity leads us to recognize our contradictions and, subsequently, the beliefs that underpin them.

Exercise:

- Take a sheet of paper or preferably a notebook and a pencil. Go to a peaceful, silent place. If this is not possible, anywhere will do providing you can concentrate.

- Sit down, close your eyes and remain silent for a few moments.

- When you feel ready, open your eyes and start making a list of your dissatisfactions, separating them according to the main areas of life: romantic relationship, friendship, family, profession, money, health and spirituality.

- Become aware of the feelings, emotions and thoughts that pass through you when you face each of these dissatisfactions. Make a short note of only one or two words beside each dissatisfaction.

- Try to remember and note down phrases that your parents or relatives used to say when you were a child that have remained with you for some reason. I am referring to rigid and generalized sentences about how life works, about you or about how people are. For example: "You'll never do well in life," "Doing what you like will not bring you any money," "This is for tramps." Phrases like these—that are normally reflexes of the behavior and attitudes of the adults in question—often transform themselves into beliefs and conditioning elements in the child's mind. They can also function in adult life as internal voices that influence how you act in relation to the world and yourself.

- When you recall some of these phrases, try to identify if there is any link between them and the contradictions you can recognize. Try to make a connection between the cause and the effect to find the beliefs that can create these contradictions. If you manage to gain access to some limiting belief acting in your system based on this identification, deepen yourself more in the observation of the feelings, sensations and thoughts that pass through you when you get in touch with this.

- Close your eyes and observe the physical sensations that pass through you when you access these memories. What do you feel in your physical body? Maybe your arms become numb, you feel heat, your heart beats faster . . . Allow yourself to feel and observe this change.

- Do the same in relation to your feelings and thoughts. What do you feel in your emotional body? For example, anger, shame or powerlessness .... Allow yourself to feel. What are you thinking at this moment? These could be phrases like "I am not loved" or "I am not good enough to accomplish this."

You can just observe, but if it is possible, go on making notes of everything, and relate this to the dissatisfaction or belief in question. We can go a little deeper at this point:

- Try to remember what you have been doing to change a certain situation that doesn't please you. Note if you are trying to do something different. And if this is the case, look at how much effort you have been making.

- Also look at what are the numbing devices that you have been using to keep yourself distant from getting in touch with these feelings. If necessary, reread the chapter that speaks about numbing mechanisms (page 49). Take note.

Key Practice 2

Freeing suppressed feelings and pacts of vengeance

As we have discussed previously, when you notice contradictions showing themselves through a negative pattern that repeats itself, creating discomfort and suffering in your life, this means there is some unconscious vengeance pact acting in your system. This aspect of lower nature is sustained by wounds and resentments—pains that have been anesthetized and denied. Every suppressed feeling and protest endured in silence and every tear unshed is an obstacle to the expansion of consciousness. This is why we need to let ourselves feel and release this pent-up pain.

The best way to reach this valley of denied feelings is to go more deeply into the practice of focused self-observation.

Begin this practice by asking yourself questions such as:

To what point do I want to develop myself?
To what point do I want to prosper and be happy? Do I really want this?

The questions can vary depending on the situation and the area of life in question. However, the crux of this exercise is to allow yourself to hear the internal voices (which you had been unaware of until then) that are constantly saying "no" to what you consciously want. If you can ask yourself honestly and have a genuine interest in finding out the truth, you will see the "no" is acting in a very practical way.

Exercise:

- Stand in front of a mirror and look deeply into your eyes. Stay like that for a few moments and then start talking to yourself about all the good things you want in your life. For example: "I want a boyfriend," "I want a car," "I want to have a great position in my company," "I want to have a company."

- Note the feelings that are emerging when you make these statements. Do you feel enthusiasm? Do you feel you want to go straight out and achieve this goal? Or do you feel guilty, ashamed, powerless?

- Talk to yourself like this for five minutes and then close your eyes and remain silent for a minute.

- Repeat this exercise for a few days, preferably at the same time, perhaps in the morning or before going to sleep.

When you deepen yourself into the practice of self-observation, you have the chance of getting to know and talking to the "general" who is commanding this self-destruction project so you can then understand his vengeance plan. This general could be fear, pride, lust or any other matrix of the lower self. When you identify who this general is, a self-saboteur of happiness inside you, try and hear what he has to say. Have a dialogue with him and let him tell you why he does not want happiness. He has his reasons.

When you hear these unconscious voices, you may also come into contact with the feelings that are supporting them.

Another exercise can then help you to free the feelings that emerge from this practice:

- Write a letter. These feelings usually end up being directed at a particular person, whether from the past or the present. Regardless of what this person represents to you, I suggest that you write them a letter, saying everything you feel and think—everything that you have not said in the past, everything you could not express at that time.

- Don't send the letter: this could worsen the energetic situation in question, and it is not the aim of this exercise. When you finish the letter, hold onto it for a few days until you can understand better the contents that have emerged in it. When you feel ready, i.e. when you feel that the emotions have been freed, burn the letter.

This exercise aims to open the ways to a healing process so that you can have a look at what is behind a certain negative situation in your life. This is an exercise to strengthen the observer, the one who sees the clouds and lets them pass by without identifying with them.

The focus is the present moment. You observe and don't react. (You don't relate it to the past or imagine how the future would be.) It does not matter if the thought is negative or positive. You let it go. You only watch it, remaining alert and with your heart open.

Key Practice 3

Totality in action: assuming control of your vehicle

The starting point of the process of awakening consciousness is related to the development of what I call totality in action, which is the ability of being present at each smallest movement you make—at each thought, word and action. That is when we dedicate ourselves to developing skills such as self-observation and mindfulness, since we can use these skills to occupy our own vehicle (physical, mental and psycho-emotional bodies). When we develop this totality in action, we begin taking charge of our own life since it is because we ourselves are not in the driving seat of our vehicle that makes us act in an unconscious way and, as a result, fall into vicious circles of suffering.

It is only when we occupy our own vehicle that we can drive it adequately. If the opposite is the case, we are led by unconscious impulses. These impulses are mainly destructive, as they result from traumas and feelings that were denied and have become frozen in our system. Therefore, they reflect negative aspects of the personality, which we can also call evil.

Although this evil or negativity manifests itself when we relate to other people, it always ends up backfiring on us. This happens because of the law of action and reaction. This is why when we are led by unconscious impulses, we end up being taken to unpleasant places. We repeat negative patterns that manifest themselves through various kinds of failure, losses, conflicts and multiple kinds of disturbances. This is self-sabotage: we betray ourselves precisely because our resources and skills are being used by these destructive impulses.

As we are not aware that we are not the only ones who put ourselves in negative situations, we feel helpless and weak and start believing we are victims and look for culprits for our problems. This is how the blaming game starts. It is one of the aspects that make up the root of human suffering. This is what we are calling the vicious circle.

When you see that you are trapped in this vicious circle, try to stop whatever you are doing, even if only for a few instants. Switch your attention back inside yourself, re-establish presence and take the control of your vehicle back. In this case, you can ask yourself questions such as:

Who is driving my vehicle?
Who is using my resources?
Who is thinking and acting through me?
Who is inhabiting this body?
Who am I?

Exercise:

- Before going to sleep at night, look back over your day from the moment you wake up to the moment you are back in bed again. Observe each action until you can identify the moment in which you lost presence, i.e. the moment in which you stopped occupying your own vehicle and were taken over by unconscious impulses.

- Repeat this exercise whenever you notice that you are absent and taken by negative impulses. By doing so, you will gradually bring to your consciousness and identify what steals your presence. It could be a situation that threatens you, a person who bothers you, a situation that causes unease, or anything else. Be aware of this and try to identify what part of your personality identifies with and reacts to a certain external stimulus, because this is the part that needs to be attentively taken care of.

You will see it is not difficult to discern who is in control of your vehicle. The question is wanting to occupy the body and regain the driving seat, but this involves detachment. To be able to detach, you need to make a conscious choice, i.e. you need to want and decide to give up the vicious circle. To do so, we need to know our pacts of vengeance before anything else. (Suggestion: study **Key Practice 2** again.)

Detachment is what allows choice, and choice allows freedom. We can only be free when we have the chance of making a conscious choice, and we can only choose this way when we are in charge of our own vehicle.

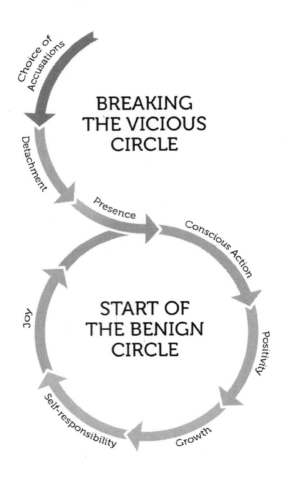

By choosing to renounce the vicious circle that perpetuates itself through our own absence, we reverse the direction of the energy that was directed towards negativity and create a new circle, a benign one.

Spirituality is synonymous with detachment. You become a spiritual person when you can detach yourself from the story you have created for yourself; when you can let go of the pacts of vengeance, the need to take the law into your own hands and the beliefs you created about what truth is. At its deepest level, spirituality is detaching oneself from suffering. Suffering is something that nobody wants but nobody gives up because it creates a sense of identity.

Attachment makes you older as you remain imprisoned to the past. Life becomes very predictable and dull because you become attached to familiar ways and settings. Even being tired of certain situations, you prefer to leave it like that because this gives you a sense of security. Detachment rejuvenates you because it opens new pathways that create the possibility of growth. Through detachment you renew and expand yourself.

When you see that you are attached to a negative situation, ask yourself:

Who am I without this impulse to argue?
Who am I without jealousy and insecurity?
Who am I without this name and story?

Key Practice 4

Identifying and removing numbing devices

Numbing devices are mechanisms we create to escape from the contact with the pain of the feelings that were denied in the past. However, this is the most direct aspect of their action. At their deepest level, numbing devices are mechanisms of escape from ourselves. This means that we lose presence and, in turn, the control of our vehicle through them. That is why the removal of the numbing devices is also essential in the process of regaining presence.

(Suggestion: re-read **Key Practice 3**)

We saw earlier that addictions and compulsions are the most obvious numbing devices, but anything can be used as a numbing device. You often don't notice you are using a certain thing or situation as a numbing mechanism.

It is not difficult to identify them. It is just a question of wanting to. And when you choose to do so, you can use your self-observation skills again.

Exercise:

- List of numbing devices: list the elements (objects, situations, feelings or emotions) that work as distractions in your daily life and steal your energy. Examples: talking on WhatsApp, surfing on social media, talking or eating too much, meeting a certain person, having a certain obsession, feeling jealous of somebody . . .

- Intelligent austerity: when you identify these numbing elements, use an intelligent austerity to remove them. Examples: try not to eat sugar or drink coffee for two or three weeks. If you feel mature enough, try to get by without any buffer.

I know it is not always easy to give up an addiction or habit, even more so when it is keeping pain hidden, so I suggest you go slowly. The removal of numbing devices needs to be done carefully because many people become desperate without them. Try not to impose impossible goals on yourself. Choose one and remove it from your list for a short period of time.

Key Practice 5

Recognizing potentials

Exercise 1: Childhood dreams

- Withdraw yourself to a quiet place with your notebook. Sit down, close your eyes and take some deep breaths.

- Visualize yourself when you were a child and try to remember how you were.

- If you wish, put on some music that opens your heart and brings back your childhood, as this can help you connect with this memory.

- Gradually try to remember those things you liked to do. Playing, games, amusements, friends .... Remember the dreams and desires you had when you were a child. The focus of this exercise is on the good things.

- Based on this memory, make a list of your main dreams. What did you want to be when you grew up? What did you want to achieve?

This list gives you clues about your gifts and talents. See if your childhood dreams are related to the activity you chose as a profession. Do you still like to do certain things you liked then? Have you been dedicating time to the things you like to do?

Exercise 2: Achievements

- List three achievements you consider a success in your life.
- List the qualities or virtues you used to achieve this. Example: courage, trust, surrender, willpower, enthusiasm, joy.
- List your skills and knowledge, i.e. everything that you have learned and studied.
- List your gifts and talents. The gift is what you do naturally, without any effort, and talent is a gift that has been refined.

Key Practice 6

Praying to awaken love

Prayer is a very powerful instrument that can and should be used by those who are seeking healing and expansion of consciousness. Prayer from a sincere soul has great healing power, individually and collectively. On praying truthfully and with purity, you emit electromagnetic light waves that can overcome the limits of space-time.

One of the practices carried out in the *ashrams* of the spiritual lineage to which I belong, the Sachcha lineage, is called *arati* and is a prayer practice in which we ask divinity to awake in everyone and everywhere. We pray for the light of Truth to reach the heart of all those who are ready. Being ready means being open and receptive, i.e. wanting to receive since that is the only way to hear the call of the heart.

This practice is carried out in the *ashrams* at the beginning of every morning and at the end of every afternoon. However, it can also be done at home once a day or when you feel it is appropriate. The main prayer used in these daily meetings is the following mantra:

PRABHU AP JAGO
PARAMATMA JAGO
MERE SARVE JAGO
SARVATRA JAGO

"God awaken! God awaken in me. God awaken in everyone and everywhere."

Exercise:

- Repeat the mantra daily for a few minutes. You can sing it accompanied by a musical instrument or just your voice. Or you can also repeat it internally, in silence, when you carry out your daily activities. It can also be used at the beginning of your daily meditation to prepare the energetic field.

- Practice this for a fixed period of time (minimum of 21 days) and see what happens. Your body is your laboratory. Carry out your experiments.

These words in Sanskrit have a tremendous power—a power that cannot be described as it is something that needs to be experienced. It is not enough to believe—you need to experience this power.

Some phonetic combinations form sounds that activate certain energetic cores in our system. A lot of research has been carried out in this area, particularly related to the old languages, such as Sanskrit. These sounds act on our nervous, endocrinal and psychophysical systems through resonance. Like a sound that can break glass when it reaches a certain pitch, these sounds can dissolve energetic blockages.

Even if we do not know the meaning of these words, they act on our system and lead us to undergo experiences the mind cannot explain. However, when we learn the meaning of the words, the mantras not only activate and transform energetic aspects but also become a prayer that can activate and transform emotional aspects.

You don't need to believe in anything to do this prayer, not even in God because God is also a word—a word that tries to explain the Mystery, the essence of which is love, the Mystery of love. You may not even believe in love. Perhaps you have never loved. Perhaps you have felt a breeze, some scent of the perfume of love that has arisen in relation to a person, someone who awakened a feeling in you that cannot be translated into words but which lifts you, gives you an opening and makes you experience things you did not believe could exist until then. The feeling of this breeze makes you happy for no reason and you trust for no reason. You want to see wellbeing in the other person and you cheer for them, often without even having any reason for doing so. It is something that defies logic.

When we repeat this mantra, we are invoking the awakening of love. Deep down, we are saying "awaken, love" as we know it is asleep. When we allow ourselves to live this experience in which we enter into communion with the Being, our heart opens up and love flows generously without wanting anything in return. This experience occurs in a field which is beyond the mind and which I call "Grace." You cannot explain why, but suddenly you are loving. Suddenly, you are happy, savoring the sweetness of a fruit you had never known before.

Peace is born from love. It is a mature fruit of the tree of consciousness. However, this tree needs to be planted and cultivated. Silence and repetition of mantras are instruments that can be used for this cultivation, but the experience of peace, which is the flavor of the fruit, is not something that can be controlled. The mind cannot control this experience—it is a flowering. You prepare the field, plant the seeds and continue cultivating them even without knowing when the tree will bear fruit.

Key Practice 7

Praying to become a pure channel of love

Prayer is not only a powerful healing instrument but also a way of exercising surrender. However, surrender is not something that can be done but something that simply happens. You cannot "surrender yourself." You can only prepare the ground so that surrender occurs. Surrender is synonymous with full trust. This means there cannot be surrender without trust. If you have surrendered, you are not shaken by outside circumstances. No matter how difficult the situation is, you trust as you know this was the way the Mystery found to fulfill the higher purpose.

When trust manifests itself at this level, you free yourself from fear, hate and all evil. You become a pure channel of love, and selfless service occurs spontaneously. However, what you can do until you have attained this level of surrender is plant seeds of trust. As well as dedicating yourself to self-knowledge, you can also use prayer as a way of cultivating trust and preparing the ground for surrender.

One of the most ancient Christian prayers says: "May Thy will be done." If we stop to think about this phrase, we see it contains the essence of surrender. This is the same as saying: "May I become a channel of Your will".

Exercise and prayer:

- Close your eyes and become silent for a minute.
- Breathe deeply a few times and begin to pray spontaneously, establishing a dialogue with the Mystery through some questions:

  What do you want from me?
  What do you want me to do?
  Where do you want me to be?

- Reflect for a few moments and, if possible, start meditating for a few minutes. The answers to these questions are inside you but you are not always ready to hear them, precisely because you are not ready to surrender. Continue reflecting:

  What is preventing me from being a channel of love?
  What am I afraid of? Why can't I trust?

- Then pray spontaneously. Continue conversing with the divinity, asking to be enlightened by comprehension and to become a channel of Its love.

Suggested prayer:

"May I be one with you. May every word that comes from my mouth be an expression of your holy word. May each deed of mine be the expression of your holy will. May our connection never be broken and may *I be able to be a channel of your love*."

DIALOGUE

Prem Baba, now that the seasonal meetings with you have ended, it's time to go home, back to the daily routine of real life, and I'm a bit concerned. Here we have daily prayer practices, yoga, and meetings with you. This is wonderful, but I don't know how to keep this same frequency at home in my daily life.

Prem Baba: I think this is a highly significant issue that raises some insights. First of all, what you're calling "real life" is a lifestyle you created and have started to see as your real life. You drew this scenario, you wrote this script you are acting out and you are now feeling a prisoner in this story since you can't see life in any other way.

But if you're the author of the play, you can alter the text. It is you who write the story and give it meaning. Maybe you don't know you have this power and that's why you believe you are a victim of circumstances, but this is happening because you're being guided by the unconscious. And this guidance by the unconscious is what you have been calling "destiny." Your vehicle is being driven by unconscious impulses, taking you from one side to the other, and you feel yourself powerless to change this.

Although we are ruled by an inescapable law of action and reaction, that decides where we stop at certain points of the journey to resolve outstanding issues from the past, this does not occur for a moral but a mechanical reason. As Isaac Newton said, every action has an equal and opposite reaction.

Our thoughts, words and actions create what we call reality. Therefore, we ourselves create the situations for life, whether they are comfortable or unpleasant, happy or undesirable. And when we are aware that we ourselves are creating unhappy situations for our lives, we can begin to transform them. Perhaps the first step to carry out this transformation is to learn to be patient in terms of where we are at this moment because *karma* sometimes still doesn't allow things to be any different. If you planted a seed and cared for it until it became a sapling or a tree, you need to handle what you planted before anything else.

For example, if you have brought a child into the world, you need to handle him. You need to honor your commitment. If you have a family and feel you are responsible for it then you need to reach an agreement about this. If you have a job and bills to pay, you cannot simply abandon everything. At the same time, this does not mean that you will not be able to realize your desires. Everything can be changed. Even when *karma* is very rigid, if you are aware of what you need to learn, you can become flexible, even if it's in the way you see the situation.

Therefore, the most important thing of all is to be aware of where you want to be and why you are in a certain situation. This is because sometimes you are a prisoner in a cell made of imagination and sometimes you are really a prisoner through the force of *karma*. In this case, you need to be creative and use intelligence to transform the situation but this creativity and this intelligence can only reach you if you open yourself up to the meaning you want to give to your life.

What is the meaning of your life? You are here to fulfill something. You have a program to perform in this incarnation. By becoming aware of your program, you move in this direction. And you will only be at peace when you can realize the program of your soul through your gifts and talents, regardless of where you are.

Some people are confident and certain that they need to be at the center of the matrix, in the big city centers, because their internal program decides they should be there to undertake certain services. Nonetheless, your program can be more flexible and you can perhaps exercise your purpose in different places.

The question is: Why are you where you are? Do you want to be where you are putting yourself? Remember it's you who are putting yourself in this place.

If you are not happy with this place, you have three possible choices: go away; stay and transform the situation; or to accept and suffer patiently. This last choice means you have to stop complaining as you have chosen to accept the situation.

Another insight that needs to be focused on in this question you have brought up is the feeling of powerlessness in the face of what you are calling destiny. When you're not in charge of your own vehicle, this means you're being guided by unconscious forces and have no idea where they are taking you. If your heart is leading you, you also don't know where but you go happily. This is the difference. When the small self is leading you, you always go with fear and insecurity and think something is wrong.

If you are not totally present in the action, you are taken by unknown forces—internal and external. You are guided by the stars, by the collective unconsciousness or even by the witchcraft done by your neighbor. In fact, you are guided by your own witchcraft because it is you who is doing this and you are doing so because you left the driver's seat of your vehicle and let anyone else take over.

What takes you to be in this place you are in today? Are you there because your heart is guiding you? Are you aware of any greater reason for being there? Or you are in this place because you are afraid of doing things differently? Are you there because of vengeance, hate, self-will? What is the reason for you to be where you are?

Regardless of where you are, whether in an *ashram* or at the center of a matrix, the way of maintaining the connection is the same: by being present, making every group of actions a prayer, transforming your life into a prayer. However, you can only do this if you are aware of the purpose of your actions.

If you are aware that you are in the matrix for the purpose of serving, you live joyfully. Even though there are difficult moments, in which the collective cruelty influences your energetic field, if you are conscious of the purpose of being there, if you are aware of being in this place precisely to help purify and transform this collective shadow, you will not fall.

At times like this, I suggest that you use some tools: get in contact with nature, even if it's just a public square; put aside some time to remain in silence and to pray; listen to mantras and chant them; carry out physical exercises; and keep good humor.

The mantra acts on the physical, emotional and mental levels through its resonance. Its phonemes operate on certain cores of the nervous system, even when you don't know the literal meaning of the words.

If you have not received a spiritual initiation and a mantra, I suggest you use the *Gayatri* or the *Prabhu ap Jago*. This is because, although they were born in the cradle of the Hindu tradition, they are universal prayers.

Gayatri:
OM BHUR BHUVAḤ SWAḤA
TAT SAVITUR VAREÑYAM
BHARGO DEVASYA DHĪMAHI
DHIYO YONAḤ PRACHODAYĀT

Prabhu ap Jago:
PRABHU AP JAGO
PARAMATMA JAGO
MERE SARVE JAGO
SARVATRA JAGO

These are some tools that can help you, but the consciousness of purpose, the awareness of service, is what is most important. Are you aware that you are serving? If you are, then your gifts and talents will be used for the great Mystery. By truly putting yourself at service, you enter the chain of happiness. Love passes through you to reach the other. This holds you and it doesn't matter where you are.

Sometimes the great Mystery can be demanding with you and ask you to be in challenging places. It asks you to give more than you believe you have. This is part of a divine game to take you from the mind. And when you are beyond the mind, you become a channel of power in which everything becomes possible.

Where does the Mystery want you to be?

At the present moment. And this present moment often means being in some place, doing something. And if you are aware of being in this place for a greater reason, you are happy.

However, if you are being driven by unconscious forces, perhaps you will be taken to places you don't want to go, to different places from where purpose would take you. This then creates an internal split that translates into anguish, confusion, sadness, depression—a series of difficulties.

Depression is due precisely to this split. Your soul wants to take you to one place, but your conditioned mind is taking you to another. And the conditioned mind is going to another place because it wants to please, it wants recognition, it never stops wanting something.

The nature of the mind is to desire. Desire is compulsive. This compulsion and desiring consume your vitality, your health and your time. And deep down, all your mind wants is to be loved. However, it only feels really loved when it is loving. At some point, you will need the courage to break with this vicious circle.

I've been trying to find my gifts, talents and mission for many years without success. I found a very deep anger that I feel towards God yesterday, an anger for Him, who is the "Almighty," because He has chosen to create such harsh laws that lead creatures to suffer so much to learn to be happy. This experience gave me a shock. Being angry with God is a dreadful sin in all religious traditions and subject the creature to terrible punishment. However, this is the truth I now see in myself. How can I leave this?

Prem Baba: At some point you heard that God lives within you and you quite probably believe this. However, you have now discovered that, deep down, you think God is outside you and that He is a demanding controller, a cruel tyrant who does not hesitate to punish you and make you suffer.

Most people in this world have this feeling, which is reinforced by different religious traditions as they teach us to fear God. This feeling is related to an even deeper belief and it is the unfolding of an image that is frozen in your system. This image is related to the figure of authority.

The first impressions of authority when a child begins to discover life's adventure come from its parents and it ends up projecting these impressions onto the image of God.

This is a very profound topic because it is also related to one of the greatest powers of the Being, which is faith. If you have a distorted view of God, your faith is also distorted. You have believed for a long time that you know what God is and you have believed that you have faith in Him. This gives you relative security and comfort because even though it is a belief and faith in a belief, you don't feel alone, even if your company is an illusion created by the mind, a fantasy created by the mind. This allows you to feel accompanied. However, at some point, due to the natural process of evolution, you are led to question this belief and this faith that is essential for you to continue your evolutionary journey. We are talking of the stages of the relationship with this Mystery we call God.

The being does not think about this until a certain stage in the process of the evolution of consciousness. It simply lives without questioning the phenomena of nature and the purpose of life. Nevertheless, consciousness naturally evolves and a time comes when it begins to ask questions. How is all this possible? Who created this reality? Why are we living this experience?

It is very difficult not to believe in a creator, up to a certain moment. Then you start to believe in the existence of a God but as you have no contact with this creator, you to start to imagine how he is. You create an image and project the image of your parents onto it as they represent the figures of authority in your life. You have built an image of God based on your memories of the past. If your parents were good, caring and welcoming, that is how you will visualize God, but if your parents were punitive, hard and cruel, that is how you will visualize God.

As our society has been governed for over ten thousand years by the distorted masculine, the main feature of which is violence and domination through the abuse of power, we obviously tend to portray God in this distorted masculine way.

What upholds this distorted image of God is false faith. Why false faith? Because this God you believe in does not exist. He was created by your mind to meet a need in a moment of anguish, but you have learned to live with this. Our society has been living like this for thousands of years.

However, the time comes when you are taken by suffering and led to question even the very existence of God. You discover you have no faith. You thought you had faith until a moment in your life when you were asked to face up to certain challenges, such as illness, losses, failures, depression . . . That is when you discover that perhaps you do not have that much faith in God and the contradiction comes out into the open.

Who is God for you? "Prem Baba said God is love, that God is the only life behind all names, all bodies. But where is this creature who does not save me here in my suffering?

Where is this creature who does not rescue me from this suffering I am undergoing? Who is this creature who invented such harsh laws that make me suffer so much to be able to see the possibility of happiness, to have a glimpse that it is possible to be happy in this world?"

So the energy which was being used to create a mental image of God starts being directed at creating a protective shell. This armor is made of rationalization. You try to explain everything through reason and science. You become skeptical.

However, skepticism is a very high stage of consciousness because you will inevitably look for answers when you are really bogged down in the lonely valley of skepticism. "If God did not put me in this situation, then who did? If it wasn't God then it was my father, my mother, so and so ...." You blame someone until you start to realize that it is you yourself who is putting you in this place.

You discover that your pain and resentment created a great rebelliousness that has reached the stage of blocking the expression of your gifts and talents, through which love flows from you. This was the way you found to protest about the maltreatment you received as a child, the way you chose to take revenge for being humiliated, hurt, insulted. So you start assuming responsibility and it is at this moment that you begin a healing process because you allow yourself to enter into contact with feelings that have been guarded and have the chance of releasing them. In doing so, you open space so you can have a real experience of God. You start to notice that God acts in you and through you. You discover that it is you who is choosing to pass through everything you are going through. In other words, you find out that it is not God who is punishing you but you yourself. There is a self-punishment, a self-hate that you project onto God. God does not chastise or punish—God is love. You are chastising and punishing yourself. You are simply reaping what you have planted.

I suggest you look for the voice inside you that says: "I don't want to give anything to anyone." Don't bother so much about God. Just sing, dance, meditate but don't worry so much about philosophical questions. Look for this internal voice that says: "I will not leave here. No one will take me from here." By doing so, you will be moving towards the direct and real experience of God.

Dear Prem Baba, I would like you to give a message to people over 50 who have still not found their way.

Prem Baba: This is an important question for people of all ages but, obviously, the older you are and have still not become aware of your purpose, the more bitter life becomes. Sometimes it reaches the point where the person feels there's no sense in being alive. When there is no consciousness of the purpose and the individuals are young, they still have lots of energy and manage to occupy time and distract themselves more easily. However, some distractions lose their attraction with time and if there is still no awareness of the purpose, it starts becoming very difficult to awaken the person. Many people who are in this situation eventually surrender to the numbing devices and live their lives waiting for death to arrive. Everyone does this in their own way but these individuals are always occupying their lives in futile activities.

Every human being has their own place in the world, even if they are not aware of this. But if you don't feel you really fit into your place, you can be taken over by envy, insecurity, jealousy and all the feelings that create war and lack of unity in your life. You fight without even knowing why you are fighting. You use the fight as a distraction. You distract yourself with superficial things in order not to look at what is happening inside yourself.

So if you are ready to start again, which means renewing yourself from within, I suggest you start asking your inner world questions such as: What is my place in the world? Why have I incarnated here? What have I come to do in this world? I want to see. I commit myself to see, even if it hurts my vanity.

Life has been putting a lot of professional pressure on me. I often feel isolated and insecure and not very creative or productive. The crisis and changes have brought this into my relation with work. I am thinking of changing direction and leaving design for yoga. How can I be more focused and productive? How can I overcome anguish?

Prem Baba: Pay attention to this question because I have seen many people having a professional crisis who decide to become therapists or yoga teachers as if being a yoga teacher or a therapist would resolve all their problems. I don't feel this would be the solution either. If you came here to be a yoga teacher then you will really feel as if you belong and fit in. But if you didn't come here for that reason then you will transfer the anguish. However, there is obviously a clue here as the thought of working with yoga makes you feel freer and more relieved. Maybe this is a passing stage. Maybe not. Maybe you will fulfill yourself giving yoga classes but you should not encourage false hopes to avoid new frustrations.

It's very good that you are open to new experiences and adventures but I suggest that you don't focus only on one particular point, becoming blind to anything else. You are looking for a vision. The vision of the purpose of your soul. This purpose was revealed to you when you were still a child. Every child arrives with a clarity of purpose but is led to forget with the passing of time. This is particularly so when adults do not nourish this vision because they don't believe in what the child is bringing, because they project their frustrations, insecurities and blocks onto the child. This often leads to the child's mind being conditioned and it starts not to believe this message or command it is bringing. It diverts itself from the path and a lot of time may be needed to find it again. At some point, that person loses trust in the possibility of realizing their dreams and spends their lives waiting for death to arrive.

It is important to rescue this divine memory and remember these commands that appeared when you were a child and which have been forgotten with time. Forgetfulness feeds forgetfulness and lots of other things appear on the way.

Dear Baba, I have been your student for years and have total trust in you but a seed of doubt has been recently put into my system: why are your courses so expensive? Please, answer this question so that the energy can flow freely once again.

Prem Baba: This is a question that takes us to different dimensions. Let's focus on some of them. The first is that perhaps your trust is not as total as you think. Perhaps it's better to say you have a quantum of trust but you still don't have total trust because you are not bothered by doubt when you have total trust.

Nevertheless, if you are to be filled with trust, you need to have a spiritual experience, i.e. that you really see and feel me; that you feel me and, subsequently, understand my game. If you can really see me, you will understand and, by understanding, you will be enlightened by trust. This trust removes all and any seed of doubt and ensures that all your needs will be met. It frees your system of all the fear, particularly the fear of scarcity.

Perhaps one of the aspects that is preventing you from entering this field of experience, one of the obstacles to seeing and feeling me and understanding my game, is linked to your beliefs related to the meaning of money. I'm talking about distortions related to the meaning and even the power of money. Although the perception of this game can only happen at the level of the soul, I can tell you some things.

The other point to be cleared up is that I am not here for money and I don't believe anybody is here for that reason. At the same time, we cannot deny that money is a reality in this existential plane. Although money is a consequence of the realization of the purpose for me, I need to have people around me whose purpose is to handle money. I need to have good administrators, because if I don't have them we will obviously fall under the shadow of money. And one of the signs of this shadow is the fear of scarcity and all its consequences.

In any case, I can say that eighty percent or ninety percent of my time is given freely. The daily transmissions I offer during the seasons in India and Alto Paraíso in Brazil are all free. However, we need money somehow or other if I am to be in these places during all this time and receive all these people. The material side of this work has to be supported. This is done through donations which we call *dakshina*, an ancient Vedic practice in which the disciple offers the master a voluntary donation as an act of retribution and respect to the law of payment for what is being received. There is a spiritual science behind this practice that activates the energy of prosperity, but this only works when the person really enters this channel and the channel opens up to the person.

A time comes when you are invited to understand this aspect of existence. You are invited to get to know the Mystery that, in the Hindu cosmos vision, is called Maha Lakshmi. This is the aspect or form of the Mother that provides for all your needs, that brings about everything you need to live your experience in comfort and calm. However, this experience cannot be forced. A time arrives when this study reaches you, although this is something that occurs within the intimacy of the master–disciple relationship.

Money is a very powerful energy. It can help you make the crossing or can destroy you. That is why dealing with this energy requires wisdom. However, it is part of the course of incarnation to learn to deal with it. We project a series of psycho-emotional content into this energy which is intimately related to the educational process experienced in childhood. For example, a child who did not receive affection but things, presents and material goods will link money to affectionate content. It is as if a colored lens was placed in front of reality and the child started seeing money in a distorted way, which is what prevents it from dealing with money in an objective way.

Activating the energy that occurs through *dakshina* flows on its own. I don't control anything. Some give more, others less, others don't give anything. As many people are involved, things end up balancing out, but sometimes there is not enough money to cover our needs to carry out an event like this. So I also offer retreats at a fixed price the other ten percent or twenty percent of the time. We are also beginning to offer workshops, basing the expenses on cooperative economy, a practice that is similar to *dakshina*. We suggest a minimum amount, which is the basic cost of the event, and people are free to contribute how much they want to give, i.e. as much as they think the work is worth.

By doing so, the money pays for what we need to do to bring these events about. However, as we have chosen to do many things, as a result of the spiritual demand and people's needs, sometimes there still isn't enough money. In this case, we ask Maha Lakshmi to make the money appear in another way. It's important that you know that this process of the operation is transparent. Everything appears in reports that are available for those who want them. We also have the idea of creating a "transparency portal" as soon as we have money available for that. This is a site in which all the organization's financial movements will be registered for those who are interested in having a better understanding of how it works. We are proceeding in this direction.

Furthermore, there are courses and therapies of the Path of the Heart, a psycho-spiritual method I created to offer support to those who are committed to self-knowledge and the expansion of consciousness. It's a combination of therapeutic tools that help you speed up and go through healing processes, facilitating and bringing the path forward.

I can't make donations in this case and you need to pay for your own therapy. I try to open the way and ease the path, but I can't walk for you. I am training the Path of the Heart therapists, but they can't work on a voluntary basis. So, just as you get paid for your work, the therapists also need to receive money to sustain their lives.

The self-development process needs to be sustainable, and there has to be a balance between spirit and matter for this to happen. And this balancing point is only found when you free yourself from the beliefs about money and align yourself with the divine codes of prosperity.

It's not enough to know what your purpose is. This purpose needs to be self-sustainable because you are incarnated in a body that is subject to the laws of matter. Some people try to deny the material dimension and try to separate spirituality from matter, but this is impossible. Denial is one of the main poisons for consciousness and makes it impossible for us to awaken from the dream of suffering.

In any case we are paying attention and studying new ways of working and supporting the therapeutic activities. We will gradually find a way to receive everyone. However, as money is the means of exchange on this earthly plane, someone needs to pay the bill. Even though most of the service is voluntary, some things need to be paid for. For everything to be free, someone needs to foot the bill. We are studying the possibilities, and suggestions are welcome.

I supported a project some time ago called "Psychology for All", which aimed to provide the therapeutic tools at accessible prices or free. I have received no more information since then and don't know if the project prospered but it was a good idea. However, for these good ideas to come about and become self-sustainable projects that prosper, someone needs to put in energy. Someone needs to give something.

This question raises a profound reflection in relation to the meaning of money. How are you dealing with this energy?

One of the aspects of my work is to eradicate fear of scarcity from your system so that prosperity can manifest itself through you. We are working to create a culture of peace and prosperity but people's needs have to be met if we are to have peace in our society. Peace is not possible as long as there is hunger. We, members of the human race, need to harmonize ourselves with the energy of money, without overestimating or underestimating its value.

About the Author

Sri Prem Baba was born in São Paulo, Brazil and studied psychology and yoga. He became a disciple of the master Sri Sachcha Baba Maharaj Ji, of the Indian Sachcha lineage. He splits his time between Brazil and India, where he gives lectures and offers retreats. He is also the author of *Transformando o sofrimento em alegria (From Suffering to Joy)* and *Amar e ser livre: as bases de uma nova sociedade (Love and Be Free: the basis for a new society)*. He has also written messages of wisdom which he calls the "Flower of the Day," distributed on a daily basis to thousands of people and translated into various languages.

MORE INFORMATION

For more information about Sri Prem Baba please visit:

www.sriprembaba.org/en

facebook.com/sachchaprembaba

@sriprembaba

Printed in Great Britain
by Amazon